Shopping Centers Unveiled

# Shopping Centers Unveiled

Ehsan Sheroy

Noble Publishing

# CONTENTS

INDEX 1

Chapter 1 3

Chapter 2 20

Chapter 3 35

Chapter 4 52

Chapter 5 71

Chapter 6 87

Chapter 7 101

Chapter 8 119

Chapter 9 137

# INDEX

**Chapter 1: Introduction to Shopping Centers**
1.1 Overview of the evolution of shopping centers
1.2 Historical context and the development of the modern shopping center
1.3 Importance of shopping centers in the retail industry

**Chapter 2: Types of Shopping Centers**
2.1 Regional malls, community centers, power centers, and specialty centers
2.2 Emerging trends in mixed-use developments
2.3 Impact of e-commerce on different types of shopping centers

**Chapter 3: Design and Architecture**
3.1 The role of design in creating a welcoming shopping environment
3.2 Notable architectural trends in modern shopping centers
3.3 Successful and innovative designs

**Chapter 4: Tenant Mix and Leasing Strategies**
4.1 Importance of a diverse tenant mix
4.2 Strategies for attracting and retaining tenants
4.3 The impact of anchor tenants on the success of a shopping center

**Chapter 5: Technology Integration in Shopping Centers**
5.1 The role of technology in enhancing the shopping experience
5.2 Use of augmented reality, virtual reality, and smart technology
5.3 E-commerce integration and click-and-collect services

**Chapter 6: Sustainability in Shopping Centers**
6.1 Green building practices in shopping center construction
6.2 Sustainable operations and energy efficiency

6.3 Consumer preferences for eco-friendly shopping destinations

**Chapter 7: Marketing and Branding**
7.1 Creating a strong brand identity for shopping centers
7.2 Marketing strategies to attract shoppers and tenants
7.3 The role of social media and digital marketing in promoting shopping centers

**Chapter 8: Challenges and Future Trends**
8.1 Common challenges faced by shopping centers
8.2 Trends shaping the future of shopping centers, including experiential retail
8.3 Strategies for staying competitive in a changing retail landscape

**Chapter 9: Success Stories**
9.1 In-depth analysis of successful shopping centers around the world
9.2 Lessons learned from both thriving and struggling shopping centers
9.3 Final thoughts on the future of shopping centers and their role in the retail industry.

# Chapter 1

## Introduction to Shopping Centers

Malls have for quite some time been vital parts of metropolitan and rural scenes, filling in as multi-layered centers that take special care of different customer needs. These powerful spaces have developed altogether throughout the long term, reflecting changes in cultural inclinations, monetary designs, and mechanical headways. As focal hubs of business movement, malls envelop an expansive range of retail outlets, diversion settings, eating foundations, from there, the sky is the limit. This exposition digs into the diverse domain of retail plazas, investigating their verifiable roots, financial ramifications, compositional elements, and the groundbreaking effect of innovation.

**Verifiable Roots:**

The idea of a concentrated commercial center has old starting points, following back to old developments where commercial centers were dynamic spaces for exchange and social collaboration. Nonetheless, the advanced mall as far as we might be concerned today has its underlying foundations in the late nineteenth and mid twentieth hundreds of years. The development of retail chains and the development of metropolitan populaces provoked an interest for more coordinated and combined retail spaces.

The Gruen Impact, named after engineer Victor Gruen, assumed a vital part in forming the cutting edge mall. Gruen imagined these focuses as business spaces as well as friendly and local area centers. The Southdale Center, which opened in Edina, Minnesota, in 1956, is many times thought about the primary encased shopping center. This noticeable a defining moment in retail engineering, establishing the groundwork for the encased, environment controlled malls that became omnipresent in the last 50% of the twentieth hundred years.

**Financial Ramifications:**

Malls are not only blocks and mortar structures; they are dynamic elements that impact and are affected by financial variables. One critical effect is on business. These focuses produce various positions, from retail staff and security work force to administrative jobs. The variety of business potential open doors inside retail outlets adds to nearby economies, turning out revenue and solidness for innumerable people.

Moreover, the presence of retail plazas can reshape the metropolitan and rural scenes. The advancement of these focuses frequently prompts expanded property estimations in the encompassing regions, driving financial development. On the other hand, the downfall of a retail outlet can make unfavorable impacts, adding to metropolitan curse and financial slumps in specific areas.

According to a buyer viewpoint, retail plazas offer a helpful one-stop objective for different requirements. The range of stores, administrations, and conveniences establishes a climate where buyers can proficiently satisfy numerous necessities in a solitary visit. This accommodation factor has added to the getting through ubiquity of retail outlets across various segment gatherings.

**Compositional Highlights:**

The engineering of retail outlets is a critical viewpoint that shapes both the visual allure and usefulness of these spaces. The format, plan, and conveniences are painstakingly wanted to improve the general shopping experience. The change from outdoors markets to encased shopping centers denoted a huge change in plan standards.

Encased shopping centers frequently highlight a focal chamber encompassed by retail spaces, establishing an organized and controlled climate. This plan not just furnishes customers with a protected and environment controlled space yet in addition works with simple route. The game plan of stores is vital, with anchor inhabitants, commonly huge retail chains, decisively positioned to draw in people strolling through and make a point of convergence.

The tasteful allure of malls is likewise a key thought. Draftsmen and planners endeavor to make outwardly engaging spaces that attract guests. The utilization of regular light, indoor finishing, and workmanship establishments add to a lovely and drawing in environment. Furthermore, the consolidation of sporting facilities, for example, food courts, play zones, and diversion scenes, adds a component of relaxation to the shopping experience.

As of late, there has been a developing pattern towards blended use improvements that join private, business, and sporting spaces. This coordinated methodology means to make dynamic, independent networks where people can reside, work, and shop inside nearness.

**Innovation's Extraordinary Effect:**

The appearance of innovation has significantly influenced the retail scene and, thusly, the plan and working of malls. Web based business, driven by headways in computerized innovation, has arisen as an impressive contender to customary physical retail. Retail outlets, perceiving the need to adjust, have embraced innovation to upgrade the client experience and remain cutthroat in the computerized age.

One remarkable mechanical incorporation is the utilization of information investigation. Malls influence information to figure out customer conduct, inclinations, and patterns. This data is significant for retailers, assisting them with fitting their contributions and advertising techniques to line up with customer assumptions. Also, information examination help retail outlet the board in upgrading the design and occupant blend to boost people walking through and deals.

The ascent of internet shopping has incited malls to investigate omnichannel procedures, obscuring the lines among physical and computerized retail. Snap and-gather administrations, virtual customer facing facades, and intelligent computerized shows are among the developments pointed toward giving a consistent shopping experience that joins the upsides of both on the web and disconnected retail.

The coordination of brilliant innovations is changing the actual framework of retail plazas. From shrewd lighting and environment control to computerized stopping frameworks, these advances upgrade functional effectiveness and supportability. Shrewd structures with interconnected frameworks empower ongoing checking and control, making a more responsive and energy-proficient climate.

Expanded reality (AR) and augmented reality (VR) are likewise tracking down applications in malls. These vivid advances offer inventive ways for retailers to draw in with clients. Virtual take a stab at encounters, intuitive item shows, and AR-improved wayfinding are only a couple of instances of how these innovations are reshaping the in-person shopping experience.

**Difficulties and Transformations:**

Regardless of their getting through notoriety, retail outlets face a bunch of difficulties in the contemporary scene. The multiplication of internet business, changing shopper inclinations, and the effect of worldwide occasions, for example, the Coronavirus pandemic have required versatility and advancement.

One of the essential difficulties is the requirement for maintainability. As natural worries become more conspicuous, malls are feeling the squeeze to embrace eco-accommodating practices. This incorporates energy-productive plans, squander decrease measures, and maintainable obtaining rehearses. Some malls are consolidating green spaces and housetop gardens, for tasteful purposes as well as to add to biodiversity and ecological preservation.

The ascent of online business has prompted a peculiarity known as the "retail end of the world," where conventional physical retailers face terminations and liquidations. Malls should wrestle with the developing retail scene and track down ways of existing together with online stages. This has incited a reconsideration of occupant blends, with an accentuation on encounters that can't be recreated on the web, like eating, diversion, and customized administrations.

The Coronavirus pandemic highlighted the requirement for versatility. Lockdowns and social separating estimates prompted a flood in web based shopping, worsening the difficulties looked by actual retailers. Retail outlets answered by carrying out security measures, upgrading cleaning conventions, and speeding up their computerized change. The pandemic highlighted the significance of versatility and adaptability notwithstanding unanticipated disturbances.

**The Fate of Retail outlets:**

As malls explore the intricacies of the advanced retail scene, what's to come holds the two difficulties and valuable open doors. The developing job of retail plazas goes past being simple value-based spaces; they are becoming experiential objections that offer a mix of business, diversion, and local area commitment.

The idea of "retailtainment" is building up momentum, stressing the joining of amusement and recreation encounters inside malls. This incorporates theaters, gaming zones, and vivid attractions that go past customary retail contributions. The objective is to establish a climate where guests wait, mingle, and draw in with the space on a more profound level.

Virtual and expanded the truth are probably going to assume an undeniably conspicuous part in store for retail plazas. These advances offer imaginative ways of improving the shopping experience, giving intelligent and customized commitment. Virtual customer facing facades, AR-upgraded item data, and VR-controlled reproductions could become standard elements in the retail plazas of tomorrow.

The accentuation on local area building is another pattern forming the eventual fate of retail plazas. Past being business substances, these spaces are advancing into local area center points that have occasions, social exercises, and social drives. Making a feeling of spot and cultivating a local area soul can add to the drawn out maintainability and importance of malls despite developing customer ways of behaving.

Manageability will keep on being a point of convergence for retail outlets later on. From eco-accommodating plans to sustainable power sources, there is a developing acknowledgment of the need to limit the natural effect of these designs. Moreover, social obligation drives, for example, supporting nearby organizations and local area outreach programs, will be necessary to the character of future retail plazas.

The job of innovation will additionally grow, with advancements like clerk less checkout frameworks, customized shopping encounters through man-made consciousness, and improved availability through the Web of Things (IoT). These progressions plan to smooth out the shopping system, making it more proficient and customized to individual inclinations.

All in all, retail plazas have crossed an entrancing excursion from verifiable commercial centers to current, innovation driven centers of trade. Their advancement mirrors the multifaceted interchange between cultural movements, monetary elements, and mechanical advancement. From their unassuming starting points to the complicated and complex designs of today, retail plazas have become necessary parts of our metropolitan and rural scenes.

As we plan ahead, the difficulties looked by retail plazas are met with imaginative arrangements and a promise to versatility. The mix of innovation, supportability rehearses, and an emphasis on making important encounters for guests are key procedures in exploring the steadily changing retail scene. Retail outlets are not simply places to trade; they are advancing into dynamic spaces that take care of the different necessities and wants of contemporary society.

The getting through prominence of malls addresses their intrinsic capacity to adjust and rehash themselves. Whether through the joining of state of the art innovation, the advancement of manageability, or the development of local area commitment, retail outlets keep on assuming a crucial part in forming the manner in which we shop, mingle, and experience our general surroundings. As we stand at the cusp of another time in retail, the excursion of malls unfurls with the commitment of proceeded with advancement and pertinence in the years to come.

## 1.1 Overview of the evolution of shopping centers

The development of retail plazas is a powerful story that traverses hundreds of years, mirroring the consistently changing embroidery of human social orders, financial designs, and compositional developments. From humble commercial centers to rambling, innovation driven edifices, the change of these business centers reflects the advancement of purchaser conduct and cultural inclinations.

### Old Commercial centers and Early Business Centers:

The foundations of retail outlets can be followed back to antiquated commercial centers, where networks accumulated to trade products and participate in friendly cooperations. These early commercial centers were energetic centers of trade, social trade, and common exercises. The Public square in antiquated Greece and the Roman Discussion are exemplary instances of such commercial centers, filling in as essential issues for exchange, political talk, and get-togethers.

While these early commercial centers missing the mark on refinement of current retail plazas, they laid the foundation for the possibility of a concentrated space where labor and products could be traded.

The idea of a common space for business exercises endured through the middle age period, where market squares in European towns and urban communities became central focuses for exchange and social collaboration.

### Ascent of Retail chains and Development of Shopping Arcades:

The nineteenth century saw a critical change in retail with the coming of retail chains. These enormous, staggered stores offered a great many merchandise under one rooftop, giving a novel and helpful shopping experience. The development of retail chains, like Bon Marché in Paris and Macy's in New York, flagged a takeoff from the dispersed and frequently turbulent nature of customary commercial centers.

Lined up with the ascent of retail chains, shopping arcades started to show up in Europe. These covered entries, enhanced with glass rooftops and complicated design subtleties, gave a shielded and rich climate for shopping. The Galleria Vittorio Emanuele II in Milan, Italy, worked during the nineteenth 100 years, is a striking illustration of a shopping arcade that joined retail spaces with bistros, eateries, and party regions.

**The Gruen Impact and the Introduction of Encased Shopping centers:**

The mid-twentieth century denoted a progressive stage in the development of retail plazas with the coming of encased shopping centers. Draftsman Victor Gruen, frequently viewed as the visionary behind present day malls, conceptualized these spaces as more than simple retail outlets. Gruen imagined retail outlets as friendly and local area centers, where individuals could accumulate, mingle, and take part in relaxation exercises.

The Southdale Center, which opened in Edina, Minnesota, in 1956, is much of the time credited as the main encased shopping center. This obvious a takeoff from the outdoors commercial centers and shopping roads of the past. Encased shopping centers gave an environment controlled climate, offering customers an agreeable and controlled space to investigate different stores.

**Extension of Shopping center Culture and the Ascent of Anchor Stores:**

The progress of the Southdale Center set up for the multiplication of encased shopping centers across the US and then some. Shopping centers became notable images of shopper culture, highlighting an organized blend of retailers, diversion settings, and eating choices. The idea of anchor stores, huge retail chains decisively positioned to draw in people strolling through, became necessary to the plan and progress of shopping centers.

All through the last 50% of the twentieth 100 years, shopping centers became inseparable from rural living. They were spots to shop as well as friendly center points where networks accumulated for sporting exercises. The Shopping center of America, opened in 1992 in Bloomington, Minnesota, embodies the fabulous scale and different contributions that became normal for present day uber shopping centers.

**Difficulties and Changes in the 21st Hundred years:**

The 21st century achieved critical difficulties and changes in the scene of malls. The ascent of online business, filled by innovative progressions and changing purchaser propensities, represented an impressive danger to conventional physical retail. Online stages offered accommodation, assortment, and the capacity to shop from the solace of one's home, testing the charm of actual retail outlets.

The peculiarity of the "retail end times" arose as conventional retailers confronted terminations and liquidations. Retail outlets, when flourishing images of industrialism, wound up wrestling with declining people walking through and changing buyer assumptions. The accommodation of internet shopping, combined with developing inclinations for encounters over material belongings, constrained retail plazas to reexamine their techniques.

**Incorporation of Innovation and Omnichannel Retail:**

Perceiving the need to adjust to the advanced age, retail plazas embraced innovation to improve the client experience. Information examination turned into a vital instrument for grasping customer conduct, inclinations, and patterns. Malls utilized this data to improve their occupant blend, design, and advertising systems to remain pertinent in the developing retail scene.

Omnichannel retail arose as a technique to overcome any issues among on the web and disconnected shopping encounters. Malls consolidated snap and-gather administrations, virtual customer facing facades, and intuitive computerized presentations to make a consistent and coordinated shopping venture. The objective was to use the benefits of both physical and computerized retail, giving purchasers a comprehensive and customized insight.

**Effect of the Coronavirus Pandemic:**

The Coronavirus pandemic, which arose in the mid 2020s, further sped up changes in the retail plaza scene. Lockdowns, social removing measures, and wellbeing concerns prompted a flood in web based shopping, strengthening the difficulties looked by actual retailers. Retail outlets, considered trivial during lockdowns, experienced phenomenal disturbances.

The pandemic highlighted the significance of flexibility and versatility for retail plazas. Because of wellbeing concerns, retail plazas executed security measures, improved cleaning conventions, and sped up their advanced change. The emergency provoked a reconsideration of the job and motivation behind retail outlets notwithstanding moving buyer ways of behaving and the developing predominance of remote work.

**Patterns Molding What's in store:**

As retail plazas explore the difficulties of the present, a few patterns are forming their future direction. The idea of "retailtainment" is acquiring unmistakable quality, underlining the coordination of diversion and recreation encounters inside malls.

The objective is to change these spaces into objections where guests wait, mingle, and draw in with the climate past simple exchanges.

Virtual and expanded reality advances are probably going to assume an essential part in improving the shopping experience. Virtual customer facing facades, increased reality item shows, and vivid reenactments expect to give imaginative and intuitive commitment that go past conventional retail. These advancements try to make important and customized encounters for guests.

The accentuation on maintainability is another key pattern. Retail plazas are progressively embracing eco-accommodating plans, energy-productive practices, and reasonable obtaining to limit their natural effect. Green spaces, roof nurseries, and drives to lessen squander add to making all the more ecologically cognizant and mindful business spaces.

Local area building is likewise turning into a point of convergence for the fate of retail plazas. Past being value-based spaces, retail plazas are developing into local area centers that have occasions, social exercises, and social drives. Making a feeling of spot and cultivating a local area soul can add to the drawn out supportability and pertinence of malls despite developing customer ways of behaving.

All in all, the development of retail plazas is an entrancing excursion that traverses hundreds of years and mirrors the powerful idea of human social orders and financial designs. From old commercial centers to the rambling, innovation driven edifices of today, retail plazas have adjusted to the changing necessities and inclinations of buyers.

The shift from outside business sectors to encased shopping centers denoted a huge defining moment, with modelers and visionaries like Victor Gruen reconsidering malls as something other than spots to manage exchanges. The difficulties presented by web based business, changing shopper propensities, and the effect of the Coronavirus pandemic have constrained malls to advance, adjust, and rethink their parts in the cutting edge retail scene.

As malls plan ahead, the mix of innovation, accentuation on manageability, center around local area building, and the development towards experiential retail are key patterns molding their direction. The account of retail outlets keeps on unfurling, promising continuous development and pertinence in the steadily impacting universe of business and commercialization.

## 1.2 Historical context and the development of the modern shopping center

The verifiable setting and advancement of the cutting edge retail plaza are interlaced with the development of business, cultural changes, and design advancements. Looking at this excursion discloses the extraordinary stages that have molded malls into the multi-layered substances we experience today.

**Antiquated Commercial centers and Early Business:**

The underlying foundations of the cutting edge retail plaza can be followed back to old commercial centers, where networks participated in the trading of labor and products. These early commercial centers were clamoring centers of monetary action, cultivating social collaborations and social trade. In old Greece, the Public square and the Roman Gathering were critical in molding the idea of a concentrated space for exchange, legislative issues, and collective life.

During the middle age time frame, market squares in European towns became main issues for business. These spaces worked with the trading of labor and products and assumed an imperative part in forming the monetary and social texture of networks. While without the coordinated design of current malls, these early commercial centers set the preparation for the possibility of a public space for business exercises.

**The Development of Retail chains:**

The nineteenth century saw a critical shift with the coming of retail chains. These foundations, like Bon Marché in Paris and Macy's in New York, changed retail by offering a different scope of merchandise under one rooftop. This takeoff from conventional commercial centers denoted the start of a more coordinated and organized way to deal with shopping.

Retail chains took care of the changing necessities of purchasers, furnishing them with an organized choice of items in a solitary area. This shift established the groundwork for the possibility that shopping could be in excess of an exchange; it very well may be an encounter. The appeal of these enormous stores reached out past the product, including the feel and the social parts of the shopping system.

**The Ascent of Shopping Arcades:**
Lined up with the rise of retail chains, the nineteenth century likewise saw the improvement of shopping arcades in Europe. These covered sections, decorated with glass rooftops and building embellishments, gave a protected and rich climate for shopping. The Galleria Vittorio Emanuele II in Milan, tracing all the way back to 1867, is a remarkable illustration of such a shopping arcade.

Shopping arcades addressed a takeoff from the outside commercial centers, offering a more controlled and tastefully satisfying shopping experience. The arcades frequently included a blend of retailers, bistros, and social spaces, establishing a climate that went past simple business exchanges. This compositional development added to the developing idea of a concentrated shopping space.

**Victor Gruen and the Idea of Shopping centers:**
The mid-twentieth century saw a change in perspective in retail engineering with the vision of modeler Victor Gruen.

Gruen conceptualized malls as business spaces as well as friendly and local area centers. His vision was established in the possibility that malls could act as spots for recreation, social connection, and local area commitment.

The Southdale Center, which opened in 1956 in Edina, Minnesota, is in many cases viewed as the primary encased shopping center. Gruen's plan incorporated a focal chamber encompassed by retail spaces, establishing an environment controlled climate that offered customers an agreeable and controlled space. The shopping center additionally included conveniences like seating regions, wellsprings, and plant life, lining up with Gruen's vision of a comprehensive shopping experience.

**The Expansion of Encased Shopping centers:**
The outcome of the Southdale Center set up for the expansion of encased shopping centers across the US and then some. These shopping centers became notable images of buyer culture, offering an organized blend of retailers, diversion scenes, and feasting choices. The encased shopping center idea gave customers a controlled climate, safeguarded from the components, and took into consideration all year shopping.

All through the last 50% of the twentieth hundred years, shopping centers became inseparable from rural living. They were spots to shop as well as friendly centers where networks accumulated for sporting exercises. The fuse of anchor stores, normally huge retail chains decisively positioned to draw in people walking through, became necessary to the plan and progress of shopping centers.

**The Development of Super Shopping centers:**
The idea of the uber shopping center arose in the late twentieth 100 years, exemplified by projects like the Shopping center of America, which opened in 1992 in Bloomington, Minnesota. These uber shopping centers took the encased shopping

center idea higher than ever, highlighting far reaching retail spaces, a wide cluster of eating choices, diversion settings, and even carnival components.

Uber shopping centers intended to make a vivid and comprehensive experience for guests. The sheer size of these advancements added to their status as objections instead of simple retail outlets. The Shopping center of America, for example, flaunts an immense choice of retail outlets as well as attractions can imagine an indoor event congregation and an aquarium.

**Difficulties and Changes in the 21st Hundred years:**

The 21st century achieved huge difficulties for retail plazas. The ascent of online business, driven by innovative progressions and changing shopper propensities, represented an imposing danger to customary physical retail. Online stages offered accommodation, assortment, and the capacity to shop from the solace of one's home, testing the allure of actual retail plazas.

The peculiarity of the "retail end times" arose as conventional retailers confronted terminations and liquidations. Retail plazas, when flourishing images of commercialization, wound up wrestling with declining pedestrian activity and changing purchaser assumptions. The comfort of web based shopping, combined with advancing inclinations for encounters over material belongings, constrained retail outlets to reconsider their procedures.

**Coordination of Innovation and Omnichannel Retail:**

Perceiving the need to adjust to the computerized age, retail outlets embraced innovation to upgrade the client experience. Information examination turned into a vital device for grasping customer conduct, inclinations, and patterns. Malls utilized this data to upgrade their occupant blend, design, and showcasing methodologies to remain pertinent in the advancing retail scene.

Omnichannel retail arose as a system to overcome any barrier among on the web and disconnected shopping encounters. Malls consolidated snap and-gather administrations, virtual retail facades, and intuitive computerized showcases to make a consistent and incorporated shopping venture. The objective was to use the upsides of both physical and computerized retail, giving shoppers an all encompassing and customized insight.

**Effect of the Coronavirus Pandemic:**

The Coronavirus pandemic, which arose in the mid 2020s, further sped up changes in the mall scene. Lockdowns, social separating measures, and wellbeing concerns prompted a flood in web based shopping, escalating the difficulties looked by actual retailers. Malls, considered trivial during lockdowns, experienced phenomenal disturbances.

The pandemic highlighted the significance of flexibility and versatility for retail plazas. Because of wellbeing concerns, malls executed security measures, upgraded cleaning conventions, and sped up their computerized change. The emergency provoked a reconsideration of the job and reason for retail outlets despite moving purchaser ways of behaving and the developing pervasiveness of remote work.

**Patterns Forming What's to come:**
As retail outlets explore the difficulties of the present, a few patterns are molding their future direction. The idea of "retailtainment" is acquiring conspicuousness, underscoring the incorporation of diversion and relaxation encounters inside malls. The objective is to change these spaces into objections where guests wait, mingle, and draw in with the climate past simple exchanges.

Virtual and expanded reality advancements are probably going to assume a crucial part in upgrading the shopping experience. Virtual customer facing facades, expanded reality item shows, and vivid reproductions plan to give creative and intelligent commitment that go past customary retail. These advances look to make essential and customized encounters for guests.

The accentuation on manageability is another key pattern. Malls are progressively taking on eco-accommodating plans, energy-effective practices, and feasible obtaining to limit their natural effect. Green spaces, housetop nurseries, and drives to lessen squander add to making all the more earth cognizant and dependable business spaces.

Local area building is likewise turning into a point of convergence for the eventual fate of retail outlets. Past being conditional spaces, retail plazas are developing into local area centers that have occasions, social exercises, and social drives. Making a feeling of spot and encouraging a local area soul can add to the drawn out manageability and pertinence of malls despite developing shopper ways of behaving.

All in all, the verifiable setting and improvement of the cutting edge mall uncover a powerful excursion that traverses hundreds of years. From antiquated commercial centers to the rambling, innovation driven edifices of today, retail plazas have adjusted to the changing necessities and inclinations of purchasers.

The shift from outdoors markets to encased shopping centers denoted a critical defining moment, with designers and visionaries like Victor Gruen reconsidering malls as something other than spots to manage exchanges. The difficulties presented by web based business, changing shopper propensities, and the effect of the Coronavirus pandemic have constrained retail outlets to develop.

**1.3 Importance of shopping centers in the retail industry**
The significance of malls in the retail business is complex, enveloping financial, social, and social aspects. These business center points act as basic parts of the retail environment, molding purchaser conduct, driving financial development, and adding to the texture of networks. This investigation dives into the meaning of malls and their unavoidable effect on the retail scene.

**Financial Effect:**
Retail plazas assume a crucial part in driving monetary action at both nearby and public levels. The sheer volume of exchanges inside these focuses contributes essentially to the retail area's generally financial result. The assorted exhibit of organizations

working inside malls creates business potential open doors, going from retail partners and directors to security faculty and support staff.

The financial effect reaches out past direct work to incorporate the whole store network. Providers, merchants, and makers benefit from the interest produced by mall retailers, making an organization of financial reliance. This interconnected trap of organizations cultivates monetary strength and security, particularly in metropolitan and rural regions where retail outlets are unmistakable financial anchors.

In addition, malls contribute considerably to burden incomes. The local charges, deals charges, and different duties created by these business foundations add to nearby and territorial spending plans. This income, thusly, upholds public administrations like schools, foundation advancement, and local area programs, making retail plazas fundamental supporters of the monetary strength of districts.

**Purchaser Comfort and Openness:**

One of the essential allures of malls lies in their capacity to give a different scope of labor and products in a solitary, effectively open area. This comfort factor is particularly essential in the present high speed society, where purchasers esteem proficiency and efficient measures. The solidification of retail outlets, eating foundations, and diversion choices inside malls makes a one-stop objective for different requirements.

The openness of retail plazas is likewise a critical figure their significance. Situated in essential regions, these focuses are intended to be effectively reachable for a wide segment. Vicinity to private areas, public transportation centers, and significant lanes guarantees that customers can promptly get to the assorted contributions inside retail plazas, further upgrading their allure.

The comfort and openness given by malls add to the peculiarity known as the "retail grouping impact." When purchasers find a convergence of different stores in a single area, it urges them to invest more energy investigating, prompting expanded people walking through and higher deals for individual retailers inside the middle.

**Social and Local area Elements:**

Past their monetary commitments, retail outlets act as essential social and local area center points. These spaces work with social associations, setting out open doors for individuals to assemble, shop, eat, and participate in sporting exercises. The plan of retail outlets frequently incorporates collective regions, food courts, and diversion zones, cultivating a feeling of local area and shared encounters.

Retail plazas become central focuses for mingling and social trade. Occasions, advancements, and local area exercises facilitated inside these spaces add to a lively neighborhood culture. From occasional celebrations to craftsmanship shows and live exhibitions, retail outlets become dynamic fields where inhabitants and guests meet up, encouraging a feeling of local area personality.

Also, malls frequently consolidate components of neighborhood culture and style in their plan and occupant blend. This mix upgrades the middle's reverberation with the local area it serves, making a space that mirrors the inclinations and upsides of the nearby populace. This feeling of commonality and association further reinforces the social texture encompassing retail outlets.

**Retail Variety and Occupant Blend:**

The significance of malls in the retail business is highlighted by their part in encouraging retail variety and giving a stage to a shifted occupant blend. Dissimilar to independent stores, malls can oblige a scope of retailers, from huge retail chains to little store shops. This variety not just takes special care of a wide range of shopper inclinations yet additionally makes a serious commercial center inside the middle.

The idea of anchor stores, normally huge retailers decisively positioned to draw in people walking through, is a demonstration of the meaning of malls. These anchor stores act as magnets, attracting clients and making a gravitational force that benefits different retailers inside the middle. This unique occupant blend adds to the essentialness and seriousness of the retail environment.

Besides, malls frequently highlight specialty stores, specialty shops, and privately claimed organizations that might battle to flourish in independent areas. This inclusivity cultivates business venture, development, and a commercial center where customers can find exceptional and specific contributions. The capacity to house both laid out brands and arising organizations adds to the wealth and variety of the retail scene inside malls.

**Flexibility and Advancement:**

Retail plazas have exhibited an exceptional capacity to adjust and improve in light of changing shopper ways of behaving and mechanical progressions. The development from customary encased shopping centers to the coordination of innovation and experiential retail is a demonstration of their strength. The joining of information examination, online stages, and omnichannel systems mirrors a guarantee to remaining significant in the computerized age.

The versatility of retail outlets reaches out to their actual foundation too. The ascent of blended use improvements, consolidating private, business, and sporting spaces, mirrors a ground breaking approach. By broadening their contributions and embracing advancements in plan, retail plazas position themselves as unique substances fit for meeting developing purchaser assumptions.

Development inside retail outlets likewise incorporates manageability drives. Perceiving the developing accentuation on natural obligation, many retail plazas are consolidating eco-accommodating plans, environmentally friendly power sources, and green spaces. These drives add to natural preservation as well as line up with the inclinations of an undeniably eco-cognizant purchaser base.

**Difficulties and Future Viewpoint:**

While malls keep on being huge players in the retail business, they face difficulties that require key variation. The ascent of web based business, the effect of the Coronavirus pandemic, and changing shopper inclinations present significant obstacles.

Notwithstanding, these difficulties additionally present open doors for retail outlets to reexamine themselves and rethink their jobs.

Online business, frequently seen as a contender to conventional physical retail, has provoked malls to investigate omnichannel techniques. Coordinating internet based stages, snap and-gather administrations, and virtual customer facing facades permits malls to use the benefits of both on the web and disconnected retail. The collaboration among computerized and actual retail encounters is a critical road for remaining important in the developing scene.

The Coronavirus pandemic sped up patterns like remote work, internet shopping, and an emphasis on wellbeing and security. Retail outlets answered by executing security measures, upgrading cleaning conventions, and speeding up their computerized change. The pandemic highlighted the significance of flexibility and strength even with unanticipated interruptions.

The future standpoint for malls is intently attached to their capacity to embrace experiential retail. The reconciliation of amusement, feasting, and social encounters inside retail outlets changes them into objections as opposed to simple value-based spaces. Retailtainment, the combination of retail and diversion, turns into a methodology for catching purchaser consideration and empowering delayed commitment.

Manageability will keep on being a vital concentration for retail plazas. Embracing green works on, decreasing ecological effect, and adding to local area prosperity line up with developing shopper values. Retail plazas that focus on manageability satisfy corporate social obligation as well as appeal to a naturally cognizant purchaser base.

he significance of malls in the retail business is tremendous and complex. These business centers act as monetary motors, driving work, producing charge income, and supporting an organization of interconnected organizations. Their job reaches out past trade, adding to the social texture of networks by giving spaces to mingling, social trade, and local area commitment.

The flexibility and versatility of malls are clear in their capacity to explore difficulties presented by web based business, changing customer ways of behaving, and the Coronavirus pandemic. The combination of innovation, center around supportability, and accentuation on experiential retail are vital reactions that position malls for proceeded with significance in the steadily advancing retail scene.

As retail outlets plan ahead, their capacity to develop, adjust, and make convincing shopper encounters will be principal. The significance of these business centers goes past the value-based nature of retail; they are dynamic substances that shape and mirror the advancing requirements, inclinations, and upsides of the social orders they serve. The account of malls keeps on unfurling, promising continuous importance and effect in the domain of retail and then some.

The job of malls in the retail business is multi-layered, enveloping financial, social, and social aspects. As unique business center points, malls act as crucial parts of the retail environment, affecting customer conduct, encouraging financial development, and adding to the general texture of networks. This investigation digs into the different angles that characterize the meaning of malls inside the more extensive setting of the retail business.

**Monetary Importance:**

Retail plazas use significant financial impact, going about as motors of trade that drive neighborhood and public economies. The monetary effect is apparent in different aspects, starting with business age. The different cluster of organizations working inside malls, from retail foundations to eateries and specialist co-ops, adds to huge work creation. This envelops jobs, for example, retail relates, directors, security faculty, support staff, and different places that structure the foundation of these business spaces.

Besides, the financial effect reaches out along the production network. Providers, merchants, and producers are indispensable parts of the environment encompassing retail plazas. The interest created by these business foundations encourages an organization of relationship that upholds monetary strength and soundness. This interconnected snare of organizations adds to the energy of metropolitan and rural regions where retail outlets frequently act as unmistakable monetary anchors.

Besides, malls assume a significant part in creating charge incomes. Local charges, deals charges, and different duties related with these business spaces add to neighborhood and territorial financial plans. The income produced upholds fundamental public administrations like training, foundation advancement, and local area programs, making retail outlets crucial supporters of the monetary prosperity of regions.

**Shopper Accommodation and Openness:**

The essential allure of retail outlets lies in their capacity to give a different scope of labor and products in a unified and effectively open area. This comfort factor is a foundation of their importance, particularly in contemporary society, where shoppers esteem proficiency and efficient measures. Malls merge retail outlets, feasting foundations, and diversion choices under one rooftop, making a one-stop objective for different necessities.

Availability is another key component adding to the significance of malls. Situated decisively in regions effectively reachable for an expansive segment, these focuses are intended to take care of many customers. Nearness to private areas, public transportation center points, and significant lanes guarantees that buyers can promptly get to the different contributions inside retail plazas, upgrading their allure as helpful and available business objections.

The comfort and openness given by malls add to the "retail bunching impact." When customers find a grouping of different stores in a single area, it urges them to invest more energy investigating, prompting expanded people strolling through and higher deals for individual retailers inside the middle. This bunching impact makes a positive input circle that benefits the two buyers and organizations.

**Social and Local area Elements:**

Past their monetary commitments, malls act as imperative social and local area centers. These spaces work with social communications, setting out open doors for individuals to accumulate, shop, eat, and take part in sporting exercises. The plan of retail plazas frequently incorporates collective regions, food courts, and diversion zones, encouraging a feeling of local area and shared encounters.

Retail plazas become central focuses for mingling and social trade. Occasions, advancements, and local area exercises facilitated inside these spaces add to a dynamic nearby culture. From occasional celebrations to workmanship presentations and live exhibitions, retail outlets become dynamic fields where inhabitants and guests meet up, encouraging a feeling of local area character.

Also, malls frequently consolidate components of neighborhood culture and style in their plan and occupant blend. This combination improves the middle's reverberation with the local area it serves, making a space that mirrors the inclinations and upsides of the neighborhood populace. This feeling of commonality and association further fortifies the social texture encompassing retail outlets.

The people group elements worked with by retail plazas reach out past business exchanges. They become spaces for social commitment, where people and families can get to know each other. The different contributions, including diversion and eating choices, add to the production of a social climate that urges individuals to visit retail outlets for shopping as well as for shared encounters.

**Retail Variety and Occupant Blend:**

The significance of malls in the retail business is highlighted by their part in encouraging retail variety and giving a stage to a fluctuated occupant blend. Dissimilar to independent stores, malls can oblige a scope of retailers, from huge retail chains to little shop shops. This variety not just takes care of an expansive range of buyer inclinations yet in addition makes a serious commercial center inside the middle.

The idea of anchor stores, commonly huge retailers decisively positioned to draw in people strolling through, is a demonstration of the meaning of malls. These anchor stores act as magnets, attracting clients and making a gravitational draw that benefits different retailers inside the middle. This powerful inhabitant blend adds to the essentialness and seriousness of the retail biological system.

In addition, retail plazas frequently highlight specialty stores, specialty shops, and privately claimed organizations that might battle to flourish in independent areas. This inclusivity encourages business, development, and a commercial center where customers can find interesting and concentrated contributions. The capacity to house both laid out brands and arising organizations adds to the extravagance and variety of the retail scene inside malls.

The fluctuated occupant blend inside malls likewise adds to the idea of retailtainment, where shopping turns into an experiential action. Past conventional retail, the incorporation of amusement choices, feasting encounters, and social attractions improves the general allure of malls, changing them into objections where shoppers can investigate and connect past simple exchanges.

**Flexibility and Development:**

Retail outlets have shown a wonderful capacity to adjust and develop because of changing shopper ways of behaving and mechanical headways. The development from conventional encased shopping centers to the reconciliation of innovation and experiential retail is a demonstration of their versatility. The consolidation of information examination, online stages, and omnichannel systems mirrors a pledge to remaining significant in the computerized age.

The flexibility of malls stretches out to their actual framework too. The ascent of blended use improvements, consolidating private, business, and sporting spaces, mirrors a ground breaking approach. By expanding their contributions and embracing advancements in plan, retail plazas position themselves as unique elements fit for meeting developing shopper assumptions.

Advancement inside retail outlets likewise incorporates supportability drives. Perceiving the developing accentuation on natural obligation, many retail outlets are consolidating eco-accommodating plans, environmentally friendly power sources, and green spaces. These drives add to natural preservation as well as line up with the inclinations of an inexorably eco-cognizant customer base.

**Difficulties and Future Viewpoint:**

While malls keep on being critical players in the retail business, they face difficulties that require key transformation. The ascent of online business, the effect of the Coronavirus pandemic, and changing purchaser inclinations present significant obstacles. Notwithstanding, these difficulties additionally present open doors for retail plazas to rehash themselves and rethink their jobs.

Online business, frequently seen as a contender to customary physical retail, has provoked malls to investigate omnichannel procedures. Coordinating internet based stages, snap and-gather administrations, and virtual customer facing facades permits malls to use the upsides of both on the web and disconnected retail. The cooperative energy among computerized and actual retail encounters is a vital road for remaining significant in the developing scene.

The Coronavirus pandemic sped up patterns like remote work, web based shopping, and an emphasis on wellbeing and security. Retail outlets answered by executing security measures, upgrading cleaning conventions, and speeding up their computerized change. The pandemic highlighted the significance of flexibility and strength even with unanticipated interruptions.

The future standpoint for malls is intently attached to their capacity to embrace experiential retail. The coordination of amusement, feasting, and social encounters inside malls changes them into objections as opposed to simple conditional spaces. Retailtainment, the combination of retail and diversion, turns into a technique for catching shopper consideration and empowering delayed commitment.

# Chapter 2

## Types of Shopping Centers

Retail outlets, frequently viewed as clamoring centers of trade, come in different shapes and sizes, taking care of different customer needs and inclinations. Understanding the various sorts of malls is fundamental for the two purchasers looking for explicit retail encounters and organizations expecting to lay out a presence in the retail scene.

**Local Shopping centers:**
One of the most notable and pervasive kinds of retail plazas is the local shopping center. These mammoth designs, ordinarily traversing north of 400,000 square feet, house a wide cluster of retail locations, eating choices, and diversion offices. Moored by huge retail chains, for example, Macy's or Nordstrom, local shopping centers intend to give a far reaching shopping experience, frequently highlighting extravagance brands close by more standard retailers. The essential position of these shopping centers in rural or metropolitan regions draws in an expansive segment, making them a focal center for shopping and mingling.

Notwithstanding retail outlets, territorial shopping centers frequently integrate conveniences like food courts, films, and sporting facilities to improve the general shopping experience. The compositional plan of these shopping centers stresses stylish allure, establishing an enticing climate for guests. With their broad determination of stores and amusement choices, territorial shopping centers become central members in forming purchaser culture and patterns.

**Public venues:**
More modest in scale contrasted with territorial shopping centers, public venues take special care of the necessities of nearby areas and act as advantageous retail objections. Going from 100,000 to 350,000 square feet, these focuses normally highlight a blend of fundamental administrations, supermarkets, and niche stores. Public venues focus on openness, guaranteeing that inhabitants have fast and simple admittance to regular necessities.

The anchor occupants in public venues are much of the time general stores or huge drug store chains, going about as the essential draw for people walking through. These focuses encourage a feeling of local area by giving a focal area to occupants to satisfy their shopping needs while likewise working with social communications. The plan of public venues holds back nothing, a design that energizes simple route and a consistent shopping experience for supporters.

**Power Focuses:**

Power focuses separate themselves by their attention on enormous box retailers and classification executioner stores. These focuses, regularly crossing 250,000 to 600,000 square feet, are described by the presence of huge, independent stores that have practical experience in unambiguous item classifications, like gadgets, home improvement, or outdoor supplies. The design of force focuses frequently incorporates a tremendous stopping region, stressing the comfort of driving straightforwardly to the ideal store.

Anchor occupants in power habitats are significant retail players like Walmart, Target, or Best Purchase, drawing in shoppers with the commitment of broad item determinations and cutthroat evaluating. While without the assorted scope of contributions found in provincial shopping centers, power focuses succeed in giving specific products at reasonable costs. Their essential area close to parkways and significant lanes makes them effectively open, adding to their ubiquity among cost-cognizant customers.

**Outlet Focuses:**

For those looking for limits and deals, outlet focuses arise as the go-to objective. These focuses include retail locations offering limited items from notable brands. Spreading over different sizes, outlet focuses can go from more modest, strip-style arrangements to bigger, encased shopping centers. The allure of outlet focuses lies in the possibility of buying excellent products at fundamentally discounted costs.

Outlet focuses frequently grandstand brands hoping to clear abundance stock or deal selective limits on their items. The format of these focuses urges guests to walk around the different stores, uncovering bargains on apparel, adornments, and home products. While the environment might miss the mark on plushness related with territorial shopping centers, the attention on worth and investment funds makes outlet focuses an appealing choice for frugal customers.

**Way of life Focuses:**

Because of changing customer inclinations, way of life focuses have arisen as a half and half retail and diversion idea. These focuses focus on establishing a lively and tastefully satisfying climate that goes past conventional shopping encounters. Regularly outdoors and structurally assorted, way of life focuses mix retail locations with feasting choices, amusement scenes, and public spaces.

The accentuation on recreation and social commitment recognizes way of life focuses from their more customary partners. Guests can partake in a relaxed walk, eat in outside bistros, and go to occasions or exhibitions facilitated in like manner regions.

Upscale brands frequently find a home in way of life focuses, adding to the general premium environment. With their emphasis on making an encounter as opposed to only an exchange, way of life focuses take special care of buyers looking for a more comprehensive and drawing in shopping outing.

**Subject/Celebration Focuses:**

For a genuinely vivid retail insight, subject or celebration focuses take the idea of way of life focuses to a higher level. These focuses consolidate topical components and amusement choices to make a climate of festivity and celebration. The plan and engineering of subject focuses are frequently custom fitted to bring out a particular climate, shipping guests to various universes or times.

Dramatic exhibitions, occasional occasions, and intuitive showcases are normal elements in topic habitats, pursuing them a famous decision for families and vacationers. Retailers in these focuses frequently line up with the general topic, improving the vivid experience. While topic focuses may not flaunt similar broad reach items as provincial shopping centers, their interesting and enrapturing conditions put them aside as objections for those looking for diversion alongside their shopping.

**Strip Focuses:**

A natural sight along metropolitan and rural streets, strip focuses comprise of a line of associated or free stores sharing a typical stopping region. These focuses are flexible in size, going from little arrangements with a small bunch of stores to bigger setups facilitating a greater choice of retailers. Strip focuses are intended for simple access, with retail facades confronting the primary street and stopping accessible straightforwardly before the stores.

Comfort is a critical figure the outcome of strip focuses, as they take special care of the necessities of purchasers searching for speedy and bother free shopping encounters. Occupants in strip places frequently incorporate supermarkets, little niche stores, and specialist co-ops like salons or cleaners. The format focuses on perceivability, permitting bystanders to recognize and get to the ideal store without exploring a mind boggling inside.

**Crossover Focuses:**

As the retail scene keeps on developing, crossover focuses have arisen as a combination of different mall types. These focuses join components of local shopping centers, way of life focuses, and different configurations to offer an assorted and versatile retail space. The objective is to give purchasers a complex encounter that takes care of various inclinations and necessities.

Crossover focuses may include a blend of customary and experiential retail, integrating both huge anchor stores and store shops. The plan frequently incorporates open spaces for occasions and public exercises. The adaptability of half breed habitats permits them to adjust to changing customer drifts and stay pertinent in a powerful retail climate.

## 2.1 Regional malls, community centers, power centers, and specialty centers

Local shopping centers, public venues, power focuses, and specialty focuses address particular points of support in the retail scene, each custom-made to meet explicit shopper needs and inclinations. Understanding the one of a kind qualities of these mall types is fundamental for the two organizations looking to lay out a retail presence and purchasers exploring the different choices accessible on the lookout.

**Territorial Shopping centers:**

Territorial shopping centers stand as goliath structures in the retail world, flaunting extensive spaces frequently surpassing 400,000 square feet. These mammoth edifices act as complete shopping objections, lodging a wide exhibit of retail locations, feasting choices, and diversion offices. Moored by unmistakable retail chains like Macy's or Nordstrom, territorial shopping centers are decisively situated in rural or metropolitan regions, attracting a wide segment of purchasers.

The charm of provincial shopping centers lies in their capacity to give a different shopping experience, taking care of a scope of tastes and inclinations. Extravagance marks frequently share space with more standard retailers, establishing a climate where customers can investigate a wide range of contributions. To improve the general insight, local shopping centers integrate conveniences, for example, food courts, films, and sporting facilities, changing the space into a social center point for people and families.

Compositionally, provincial shopping centers focus on tasteful allure, with plans pointed toward establishing an enticing and outwardly satisfying climate. The design frequently includes roomy walkways, normal regions, and decisively positioned anchor stores to direct guests through the assorted cluster of contributions. The outcome of territorial shopping centers isn't just estimated in deals yet additionally in their capacity to shape purchaser culture and impact patterns through a cautiously organized shopping experience.

**Public venues:**

As opposed to the greatness of territorial shopping centers, public venues are portrayed by their attention on nearby areas and the comfort they bring to inhabitants. These focuses are more modest in scale, ordinarily going from 100,000 to 350,000 square feet, and mean to offer fundamental types of assistance and retail choices inside simple reach of nearby networks.

Anchor occupants in public venues frequently incorporate grocery stores or enormous drug store chains, filling in as essential draws for people walking through. The objective is to offer occupants a focal area for satisfying ordinary shopping needs, cultivating a feeling of local area by giving a space where neighbors can meet up. Usefulness is a critical thought in the plan of public venues, guaranteeing that the design works with simple route and a consistent shopping experience for benefactors.

While public venues might come up short on broad assortment of provincial shopping centers, they succeed in gathering the everyday necessities of neighborhood customers. The vicinity and availability of these focuses make them fundamental parts of neighborhood life, supporting both the comfort and social attachment of the networks they serve.

**Power Focuses:**

Power focuses arise as a particular classification inside the mall scene, zeroing in on huge box retailers and class executioner stores. These focuses, normally crossing 250,000 to 600,000 square feet, are portrayed by the presence of huge, independent stores represent considerable authority in unambiguous item classes like gadgets, home improvement, or outdoor supplies.

The format of force focuses frequently incorporates broad stopping regions, stressing the accommodation of driving straightforwardly to the ideal store. Anchor occupants in power places are significant retail players like Walmart, Target, or Best Purchase, drawing in customers with the commitment of broad item determinations and serious valuing. While power focuses may come up short on different scope of contributions found in local shopping centers, they succeed in giving particular merchandise at reasonable costs.

The essential area of force focuses close to expressways and significant lanes improves their openness, making them famous among cost-cognizant customers looking for an engaged and productive shopping experience.

The direct design and accentuation on unambiguous item classifications add to the allure of force habitats for those hoping to satisfy specific necessities without the interruptions of a more far reaching retail climate.

**Specialty Focuses:**

Specialty focuses cut a specialty for themselves by taking care of explicit shopper interests or item classes. Not at all like the expansive range of contributions in provincial shopping centers, specialty fixates center around a particular topic or market portion. These focuses can change in size and arrangement, going from little shop groups to bigger, more particular edifices.

The allure of specialty focuses lies in their capacity to give an arranged determination of items or administrations custom fitted to a particular segment or vested party. Models incorporate innovation centered focuses lodging hardware retailers or style driven focuses exhibiting top of the line architect stores. The consistent idea among specialty focuses is their obligation to conveying an interesting and designated shopping experience.

The plan and environment of specialty focuses are made to line up with the subject or specialty they address. This can include particular structural components, topical stylistic theme, and a painstakingly chosen blend of occupants. Buyers looking for a more engaged and vivid shopping experience are attracted to specialty focuses, where they can investigate and enjoy their particular advantages without the interruptions of a more extensive retail climate.

Provincial shopping centers, public venues, power focuses, and specialty focuses address the different embroidery of the cutting edge retail scene, each offering a novel mix of elements and encounters. Territorial shopping centers hold back nothing variety, giving an exhaustive shopping and mingling objective. Public venues focus on nearby comfort, becoming indispensable to the day to day routines and social texture of neighborhoods.

Power focuses have some expertise in huge organization retail, offering practical arrangements with an emphasis on unambiguous item classes. Specialty focuses cut out specialties, taking care of the interests and inclinations of designated shopper portions. Each kind of retail plaza assumes a vital part in gathering the developing necessities and assumptions for shoppers in various settings.

Understanding the unmistakable qualities of these mall types is essential for organizations meaning to lay out a retail presence, as it illuminates vital choices about area, inhabitant blend, and by and large situating. Moreover, buyers benefit from this comprehension, as it permits them to explore the retail scene with a more clear feeling of what each kind of mall offers.

In a dynamic and steadily changing retail climate, the concurrence of provincial shopping centers, public venues, power focuses, and specialty focuses mirrors the versatility of the business.

Whether looking for a great shopping experience, nearby comfort, specific contributions, or savvy arrangements, purchasers can find a mall custom-made to their inclinations, adding to the proceeded with development of the retail scene.

### 2.2 Emerging trends in mixed-use developments

In the powerful scene of metropolitan turn of events, blended use improvements have arisen as a groundbreaking power, forming the manner in which we live, work, and cooperate inside metropolitan conditions. These turns of events, portrayed by the reconciliation of different capabilities like private, business, and sporting spaces, have advanced after some time, leading to new and imaginative patterns that rethink the idea of metropolitan living.

**Obscuring Limits:**

One striking pattern in blended use improvements is the deliberate obscuring of limits between various capabilities. Customarily, improvements were compartmentalized, with particular zones for private, business, and sporting purposes. Be that as it may, contemporary blended use projects mean to separate these obstructions, making consistent changes between work, recreation, and living spaces.

This obscuring of limits isn't just physical however reaches out to the programming and plan of spaces. For instance, a blended use improvement could coordinate office spaces with common regions, establishing conditions that support joint effort and social collaboration. By eradicating the unbending differentiations between capabilities, engineers look to improve the general insight of occupants and advance a more incorporated and dynamic metropolitan way of life.

**Supportability and Green Spaces:**

As supportability turns into an undeniably fundamental thought in metropolitan preparation, blended use advancements are consolidating green plan standards to make harmless to the ecosystem and stylishly satisfying spaces. Roof gardens, green exteriors, and energy-productive innovations are essential components of these turns of events, encouraging a harmonious connection between the constructed climate and nature.

Reasonable blended use projects frequently focus on energy productivity, squander decrease, and the utilization of sustainable assets. The combination of green spaces not just adds to the general prosperity of inhabitants yet in addition upgrades the natural impression of the turn of events. These drives line up with the developing attention to natural worries and the longing to make metropolitan spaces that are both practical and biologically dependable.

**Tech-Driven Conditions:**

In the time of brilliant urban communities and computerized availability, blended use improvements are embracing innovation to upgrade the personal satisfaction for occupants and clients. From shrewd home frameworks and energy the board answers for cutting edge security highlights, innovation assumes a crucial part in molding the cutting edge blended use insight.

Tech-driven conditions in blended use advancements stretch out past individual living spaces. Shrewd framework, like brilliant stopping frameworks and coordinated transportation arrangements, adds to the proficiency and accommodation of these metropolitan spaces. Furthermore, the incorporation of increased reality (AR) and augmented reality (VR) innovations is changing the manner in which designers plan and market blended use projects, furnishing expected occupants with vivid encounters and virtual visits.

**Adaptable Plan and Versatile Reuse:**

Adaptability in plan and versatile reuse are arising patterns that highlight the flexibility of blended use improvements. As opposed to sticking to static, foreordained plans, engineers are integrating adaptable plan rules that consider changes in view of developing necessities and patterns. This flexibility guarantees that blended use spaces stay pertinent and receptive to the changing elements of metropolitan life.

Versatile reuse, an idea established in maintainability, includes reusing existing designs for new capabilities. This pattern has gotten forward movement in blended use advancements, where notable structures or modern spaces are changed into lively center points that consistently mix the old with the new. This jam structural legacy as well as adds an exceptional person to blended use projects, making spaces with a rich feeling of history and variety.

**Accentuation on Health and Local area:**

Wellbeing has turned into a focal concentration in present day blended use improvements, mirroring a more extensive cultural shift towards better ways of life. Designers are consolidating health conveniences, for example, wellness focuses, reflection spaces, and wellbeing zeroed in retail outlets to advance physical and mental prosperity. Furthermore, the combination of nature-motivated plan components adds to a quieting and reviving climate inside these turns of events.

Local area building is one more huge pattern inside blended use projects. Past giving actual spaces to inhabitants to live and work, designers are setting out open doors for social connection and local area commitment. Normal regions, occasion spaces, and mutual nurseries are intended to encourage a feeling of having a place and network among occupants, laying out blended use improvements as spots to occupy as well as lively networks where people can shape significant associations.

**Comprehensive and Open Plan:**

Inclusivity and openness have acquired unmistakable quality as fundamental contemplations in the plan of blended use improvements. The objective is to make spaces that take care of different socioeconomics and guarantee that everybody, paying little mind to mature or capacity, can completely partake in and partake in the advantages of metropolitan living.

This pattern incorporates highlights, for example, widespread plan standards, which expect to establish conditions that are open to people with fluctuating degrees of portability. Comprehensive plan likewise stretches out to the blend of conveniences and administrations inside a turn of events, guaranteeing that the requirements of different populaces, including families, seniors, and people with handicaps, are tended to.

**Center around Localism and Validness:**

Blended use improvements are progressively embracing a feeling of localism and credibility, drawing motivation from the novel person and social character of the encompassing local area. Engineers are consolidating nearby materials, building styles, and social impacts to make spaces that reverberate with the set of experiences and character of the area.

This pattern isn't restricted to feel; it reaches out to the blend of organizations and administrations inside a blended use improvement. Privately claimed shops, high quality business sectors, and local area driven drives add to the formation of legitimate, neighborhood-driven spaces. By celebrating neighborhood culture and cultivating an association with the local area, blended use improvements become something other than structures; they become indispensable pieces of the social texture.

**Incorporation of Collaborating Spaces:**

As the idea of work goes through a change in outlook towards expanded adaptability and distant joint effort, blended use improvements are consolidating cooperating spaces to meet the developing necessities of occupants. These common work areas give a helpful and cooperative climate for experts, specialists, and telecommuters.

The joining of collaborating spaces inside blended use improvements not just adds a layer of comfort for occupants yet in addition adds to a more powerful and different local area. Shared conveniences, meeting rooms, and systems administration occasions set out open doors for coordinated effort and information trade, cultivating a feeling of expert local area inside the more extensive private setting.

**Blended Use Advancements as Social Centers:**

In a takeoff from the customary perspective on blended use improvements exclusively as private or business spaces, there is a developing pattern of situating these advancements as social center points. This includes the joining of social foundations, craftsmanship exhibitions, execution spaces, and instructive offices inside the texture of blended use projects.

By meshing social components into the plan and programming of these turns of events, designers expect to make improving encounters for occupants and guests the same. Social centers inside blended use projects add to the dynamic quality of metropolitan life, cultivating inventiveness, scholarly commitment, and a feeling of social personality inside the local area.

The advancement of blended use improvements mirrors the unique exchange between urbanization, cultural patterns, and the changing inclinations of occupants. The arising patterns in blended use improvements, from obscuring limits and maintainability to tech-driven conditions and comprehensive plan, highlight the flexibility and advancement inside the domain of metropolitan preparation.

As blended use improvements keep on molding the metropolitan scene, these patterns mean a takeoff from conventional models of city arranging and land improvement. They address a shift towards additional all encompassing, human-driven approaches that focus on supportability, prosperity, and local area. In exploring the eventual fate of metropolitan living, these patterns act as guideposts, forming the up and coming age of blended use advancements that consistently coordinate into the texture of our developing urban areas.

## 2.3 Impact of e-commerce on different types of shopping centers

The coming of online business has achieved a change in outlook in the retail scene, on a very basic level modifying the manner in which customers shop and reshaping the elements of customary malls. The effect of online business fluctuates across various sorts of retail plazas, from provincial shopping centers to public venues, power focuses, and specialty focuses. Understanding these impacts is essential for both the retail business and shoppers as they explore an undeniably advanced commercial center.

**Territorial Shopping centers:**

Territorial shopping centers, when considered strongholds of in-person retail encounters, have confronted the two difficulties and open doors following the online business blast. On one hand, internet business has represented a danger to conventional physical retailers inside provincial shopping centers, with purchasers progressively selecting the comfort of web based shopping. This change in shopper conduct has prompted the conclusion of certain stores and a decrease in people strolling through inside these sweeping retail plazas.

Be that as it may, local shopping centers have additionally perceived the need to adjust and use internet business for their potential benefit. Numerous customary retailers working inside these shopping centers have laid out web-based stages, giving purchasers the choice to shop carefully while keeping an actual presence. Also, provincial shopping centers have embraced the idea of "snap and-gather," permitting clients to arrange on the web and get their buys at assigned areas inside the shopping center. This combination of on the web and disconnected channels looks to upgrade the general shopping experience and overcome any barrier between customary retail and internet business.

The job of provincial shopping centers is developing past unadulterated retail, with an expanded spotlight on making experiential objections. Shopping centers are consolidating diversion choices, feasting encounters, and other recreation exercises to draw in guests past the customary shopping schedule.

This broadening plans to offset the effect of web based business by giving an exceptional and participating face to face experience that can't be recreated on the web.

**Public venues:**

Public venues, intended to take special care of the requirements of nearby areas, have felt the impact of online business in particular ways. The comfort of web based shopping has impacted the interest for ordinary labor and products normally found in public venues, for example, supermarkets and little niche stores. Buyers, drawn by the simplicity of computerized shopping, may settle on web-based staple conveyance benefits instead of visiting the nearby general store.

Notwithstanding, the effect of internet business on public venues is nuanced. Some public venues have effectively adjusted by embracing internet business themselves. Nearby organizations inside these focuses have laid out web-based customer facing facades, offering inhabitants the comfort of computerized shopping while at the same time holding an association with the area. Furthermore, public venues are zeroing in on giving encounters that go past simple exchanges, cultivating a feeling of local area through occasions, get-togethers, and customized administrations that web based business stages might battle to repeat.

The people group driven nature of these focuses benefits them, as occupants frequently esteem the nearness and individual hint of nearby organizations. Internet business has provoked public venues to investigate imaginative systems, for example, curbside pickup and nearby conveyance administrations, to rival the comfort presented by online stages.

**Power Focuses:**

Power focuses, with their accentuation on huge box retailers and classification executioner stores, have encountered the two difficulties and strength notwithstanding web based business. On one hand, the comfort and immense item determination presented by web based business monsters can represent a danger to the specific retailers inside power habitats. Purchasers might decide to peruse online commercial centers for explicit items as opposed to visiting individual stores in a power place.

Nonetheless, power focuses enjoy specific benefits that moderate the effect of web based business. The actual presence of huge retailers, frequently offering cutthroat estimating and many items, can draw in clients who lean toward an in-person shopping experience. Also, the essential arrangement of force focuses close to roadways and significant lanes improves their perceivability and openness, making them helpful choices for customers who esteem quickness.

To stay cutthroat in the computerized age, power focuses are embracing omnichannel methodologies. This includes incorporating on the web and disconnected channels to make a consistent shopping experience.

A few retailers inside power habitats have laid out strong web based business stages, permitting clients to peruse and buy items online while utilizing the actual store for administrations like in-store pickup or returns. This mixture approach plans to catch the upsides of both on the web and disconnected retail, tending to the developing inclinations of present day purchasers.

**Specialty Focuses:**

Specialty focuses, planned around unambiguous item classes or interests, face one of a kind difficulties and open doors in the time of online business. On one hand, the comfort of internet shopping can represent a danger to specialty retailers, as buyers might pick the more extensive determination and simplicity of computerized stages. For instance, an innovation centered specialty place might find buyers floating towards online hardware retailers offering a broad exhibit of items.

Notwithstanding, specialty focuses likewise can possibly cut out a specialty in the computerized scene. The organized and centered nature of these focuses can interest buyers looking for a committed and vivid shopping experience. Some specialty retailers have effectively progressed to web based business by laying out web-based stages that reflect the organized contributions tracked down in their actual stores. This permits them to contact a more extensive crowd while keeping up with the specific allure that separates them.

The incorporation of innovation inside specialty places is one more road for variation. For example, expanded reality (AR) and computer generated reality (VR) advancements can be utilized to make virtual encounters that feature items in a dynamic and intelligent way. By utilizing these innovations, specialty focuses can give online customers a remarkable and drawing in experience that lines up with their particular advantages.

The effect of internet business on various sorts of malls is diverse, mirroring the powerful interaction between advanced development and customary retail models. While web based business has presented difficulties, it has likewise prodded advancement and transformation inside the retail business.

Provincial shopping centers are reclassifying their job as experiential objections, mixing on the web and disconnected channels to improve the general shopping experience. Public venues are utilizing their nearby concentration and encouraging local area commitment to stay strong despite computerized rivalry. Power focuses are embracing omnichannel methodologies to consolidate the qualities of enormous retailers with the comfort of web based shopping. Specialty focuses are embracing internet business while saving their specialty advance through arranged contributions and vivid web-based encounters.

In exploring the effect of web based business, malls are not just adjusting to make due; they are developing to flourish in the advanced age. The eventual fate of retail lies in a fragile harmony between online comfort and the one of a kind encounters that actual malls can give.

As the retail scene keeps on developing, the coordination of web based business and conventional retail models will shape a dynamic and versatile shopping climate that takes care of the different inclinations of present day buyers.

Malls, necessary parts of the retail scene, come in assorted structures, each taking care of explicit buyer needs, inclinations, and territorial elements. Understanding the different sorts of malls is fundamental for the two purchasers looking for customized retail encounters and organizations expecting to lay out an essential presence on the lookout.

1. **Territorial Shopping centers:**
   Territorial shopping centers are notorious, enormous scope shopping objections that overwhelm metropolitan and rural scenes. Described by their extensive size, frequently surpassing 400,000 square feet, local shopping centers house a complete blend of retail locations, feasting choices, and diversion offices. Secured by significant retail chains like Macy's, Nordstrom, or JC Penney, territorial shopping centers plan to give a sweeping shopping experience, interesting to a wide segment.
   
   These shopping centers focus on stylish allure in their compositional plan, establishing an enticing climate with open walkways, normal regions, and decisively positioned anchor stores. Past retail, local shopping centers frequently consolidate conveniences like food courts, films, and sporting spaces, situating themselves as friendly centers where buyers can shop, eat, and take part in relaxation exercises. Their essential area in clamoring rural or metropolitan regions makes them fundamental to forming purchaser culture and affecting patterns.

2. **Public venues:**
   Rather than the magnificence of territorial shopping centers, public venues center around serving the particular necessities of nearby areas. Going in size from 100,000 to 350,000 square feet, these focuses focus on availability and comfort. Moored by grocery stores or huge drug store chains, public venues

offer a blend of fundamental administrations, supermarkets, and niche stores to meet the regular requirements of neighboring occupants.

The plan of public venues underscores usefulness, giving an effectively traversable design that works with a consistent shopping experience. Past retail, these focuses expect to cultivate a feeling of local area by offering a focal social event space where neighbors can satisfy their everyday shopping necessities. With a nearby concentration, public venues add to the social texture of neighborhoods, offering fundamental types of assistance inside closeness to local locations.

3. **Power Focuses:**

   Power focuses are described by their attention on huge box retailers and classification executioner stores. Going in size from 250,000 to 600,000 square feet, these focuses focus on comfort and moderateness.

   Significant retail players like Walmart, Target, or Best Purchase anchor power focuses, attracting buyers with the commitment of broad item determinations and serious evaluating.

   The format of force focuses frequently incorporates tremendous stopping regions, featuring the comfort of driving straightforwardly to the ideal store. While coming up short on the assorted scope of contributions found in territorial shopping centers, power focuses succeed in giving particular products at reasonable costs. Their essential position close to thruways and significant lanes improves openness, making them well known among cost-cognizant customers looking for an engaged and proficient shopping experience.

4. **Outlet Focuses:**

   For deal trackers and worth cognizant shoppers, outlet focuses offer a safe house of limited items from notable brands. Traversing different sizes, outlet focuses can go from more modest strip-style arrangements to bigger encased shopping centers. These focuses draw in customers with the possibility of buying excellent merchandise at fundamentally discounted costs.

   Outlet focuses frequently include brands hoping to clear overabundance stock or proposition select limits on their items. While the air might come up short on richness related with provincial shopping centers, the attention on worth and reserve funds makes outlet focuses an alluring choice for economical customers. The design urges guests to investigate different stores, uncovering bargains on dress, frill, and home merchandise.

5. **Way of life Focuses:**

   Answering changing buyer inclinations, way of life focuses have arisen as a cross breed retail and diversion idea. Normally outside and compositionally different, these focuses mix retail locations with feasting choices, diversion settings, and public spaces. Dissimilar to conventional retail plazas, way of life focuses focus on establishing an energetic and tastefully satisfying climate that reaches out past shopping.

Upscale brands frequently find a home in way of life focuses, adding to a general premium climate. The accentuation on relaxation and social commitment recognizes way of life focuses from their more customary partners. Guests can partake in a comfortable walk, feast in outdoors bistros, and go to occasions or exhibitions facilitated in like manner regions. By zeroing in on making an encounter as opposed to only an exchange, way of life focuses take care of customers looking for a more comprehensive and drawing in shopping outing.

6. **Topic/Celebration Focuses:**
For a really vivid retail insight, subject or celebration focuses take the idea of way of life focuses to a higher level. These focuses integrate topical components and amusement choices to make a climate of festivity and merriment. The plan and engineering of subject focuses are frequently custom-made to inspire explicit ambiances, moving guests to various universes or times.

Dramatic exhibitions, occasional occasions, and intuitive presentations are normal highlights in topic places, settling on them famous decisions for families and sightseers. Retailers in these focuses frequently line up with the general topic, improving the vivid experience. While topic focuses may not flaunt similar broad reach items as territorial shopping centers, their special and spellbinding conditions put them aside as objections for those looking for amusement alongside their shopping.

7. **Strip Focuses:**
A recognizable sight along metropolitan and rural streets, strip focuses comprise of a column of associated or free stores sharing a typical stopping region. Flexible in size, strip focuses can go from little arrangements with a small bunch of stores to bigger setups facilitating a greater determination of retailers. Strip focuses are intended for simple access, with retail facades confronting the primary street and stopping accessible straightforwardly before the stores.

Comfort is a critical figure the progress of strip focuses, taking care of the requirements of purchasers searching for fast and bother free shopping encounters. Occupants in strip places frequently incorporate supermarkets, little niche stores, and specialist co-ops like salons or cleaners. The format focuses on perceivability, permitting bystanders to distinguish and get to the ideal store without exploring a mind boggling inside.

8. **Cross breed Communities:**

As the retail scene develops, cross breed communities have arisen as a combination of different mall types. These focuses consolidate components of local shopping centers, way of life focuses, and different organizations to offer an assorted and versatile retail space. The objective is to furnish buyers with a complex encounter that takes care of various inclinations and necessities.

Half breed places might include a blend of conventional and experiential retail, consolidating both huge anchor stores and store shops. The plan frequently incorporates open spaces for occasions and collective exercises. The adaptability of crossover focuses permits them to adjust to changing customer drifts and stay pertinent in a unique retail climate.

All in all, the different kinds of malls take care of a great many shopper inclinations and requirements, mirroring the developing idea of the retail scene. From the glory of territorial shopping centers to the accommodation of strip focuses and the vivid encounters of subject focuses, each type adds to the rich woven artwork of retail conditions. As buyer ways of behaving and assumptions keep on advancing, malls will without a doubt adjust and enhance to satisfy the needs of the cutting edge commercial center.

# Chapter 3

## Design and Architecture

Plan and engineering assume essential parts in molding the physical and virtual spaces we occupy, impacting style as well as usefulness, ease of use, and in general client experience. Whether in the domain of structures, programming, or UIs, smart plan and very much created engineering are essential to establishing conditions that are both outwardly engaging and practically viable.

In the domain of actual engineering, the plan of structures is a multi-faceted undertaking that envelops style, primary honesty, spatial association, and ecological contemplations. Designers should adjust structure and capability, tending to the useful necessities of inhabitants while likewise making structures that are tastefully satisfying and socially applicable. The historical backdrop of engineering is a rich embroidery of developing styles, from traditional to present day, each mirroring the social, innovative, and cultural settings of now is the ideal time.

One of the major contemplations in building configuration is spatial association. The plan of spaces inside a structure, their sizes, and their interconnections all add to the general client experience. Planners frequently utilize standards of spatial plan to establish conditions that are utilitarian as well as genuinely thunderous. The progression of spaces, the control of light, and the cautious choice of materials all add to the production of spaces that get explicit sentiments or reactions from inhabitants.

Primary honesty is one more basic part of engineering plan. Structures should be intended to endure the powers of nature, whether it be wind, seismic tremors, or other ecological variables. The selection of materials and development techniques is vital in guaranteeing a structure's strength and security. Progresses in innovation have led to imaginative primary arrangements, like the utilization of maintainable materials, shrewd structure frameworks, and parametric plan apparatuses that consider multi-faceted and effective designs.

Natural contemplations are progressively significant in present day structural plan. Feasible engineering plans to limit the natural effect of structures by integrating energy-proficient frameworks, inexhaustible materials, and eco-accommodating development rehearses. Green structure principles, like LEED (Authority in Energy and Ecological Plan), guide modelers in making structures that are naturally dependable as well as financially savvy and asset productive.

In the domain of computerized engineering, the plan and design of programming frameworks and UIs are similarly essential. Programming configuration incorporates the undeniable level design of a framework, including its parts, modules, and their communications. Very much planned programming isn't just proficient and solid yet in addition versatile to evolving prerequisites. The standards of programming engineering guide the association of code, the selection of structures, and the general construction of a product framework.

UI (UI) and client experience (UX) plan are vital in making programming that is natural and easy to use. The UI is the mark of communication between a client and a product application, enveloping all that from buttons and menus to visual design and typography. Powerful UI configuration thinks about the client's necessities, assumptions, and mental cycles to make interfaces that are stylishly satisfying as well as simple to explore.

UX plan, then again, centers around the general insight of the client all through their collaboration with an item or framework. It includes understanding client ways of behaving, leading convenience testing, and repeating on plans to upgrade the client venture. Great UX configuration goes past the visual components and considers the whole client experience, including factors like execution, openness, and the close to home effect of the communication.

The lined up among physical and computerized engineering becomes clear while thinking about the idea of data design. In the computerized domain, data design alludes to the association and construction of content inside a site or application. Similarly as a very much planned building gives clear wayfinding and consistent association of spaces, compelling data engineering guarantees that computerized content is coordinated in a manner that is not difficult to explore and comprehend.

The standards of configuration thinking, a human-focused way to deal with critical thinking, are vital to both physical and computerized plan. Configuration thinking underscores sympathy, ideation, prototyping, and testing as iterative cycles that lead to inventive and client driven arrangements. This system isn't restricted to planners; it tends to be applied across disciplines to resolve complex issues and produce intelligent fixes.

Lately, the idea of parametric plan has acquired noticeable quality in both physical and advanced design. Parametric plan includes the utilization of calculations to create and control plan components, considering a serious level of intricacy and variety. In engineering, parametric plan can be applied to make unpredictable veneers, dynamic designs, and responsive conditions. In advanced plan, parametric methods empower the formation of perplexing and versatile UIs.

The combination of innovation into design has led to the idea of "shrewd structures." Brilliant structures use sensors, robotization, and availability to upgrade the effectiveness, solace, and security of tenants. These structures can change lighting, warming, and cooling in view of inhabitance and natural circumstances, advancing energy use and making more maintainable and responsive spaces.

In the domain of computerized engineering, the approach of distributed computing has changed how programming frameworks are planned and conveyed. Cloud engineering takes into consideration versatile and adaptable arrangements by utilizing dispersed figuring assets. This shift has suggestions not just for the specialized parts of programming plan yet in addition for plans of action and the manner in which associations convey and adapt programming administrations.

The significance of openness in plan couldn't possibly be more significant, whether in the physical or advanced domain. In actual engineering, availability contemplations include planning spaces that are comprehensive and obliging to people with assorted needs, incorporating those with handicaps. Inclines, lifts, and more extensive entryways are instances of highlights that improve actual availability. In advanced plan, availability envelops planning connection points and content that can be effectively explored and perceived by people with handicaps, for example, those utilizing screen perusers or voice orders.

Moral contemplations are progressively turning into a point of convergence in plan and engineering. Planners and modelers bear an obligation to think about the social and social ramifications of their work. This incorporates resolving issues of value, variety, and consideration in both physical and computerized spaces. In the computerized domain, moral contemplations stretch out to information protection, security, and the dependable utilization of innovation.

The cooperative idea of plan and engineering is obvious in the interdisciplinary groups that meet up to carry thoughts to completion. Modelers, planners, engineers, and different experts team up to address the complex difficulties intrinsic in establishing physical and computerized conditions. Compelling correspondence and a common vision are fundamental for fruitful joint effort, whether in planning a structure or fostering a product application.

The iterative idea of the plan interaction is a consistent theme that goes through both physical and computerized plan. Prototyping, testing, and refining are necessary parts of the plan venture, permitting creators and draftsmen to gain from disappointments and triumphs the same. This iterative methodology is especially apparent in lithe techniques ordinarily utilized in programming advancement, where cross-utilitarian groups work cooperatively so, iterative cycles to convey gradual upgrades.

As innovation keeps on propelling, the limits among physical and computerized plan are turning out to be progressively obscured. The idea of the "computerized twin" epitomizes this combination, wherein a computerized portrayal of an actual item or framework is made to recreate, screen, and examine its certifiable partner. In engineering, advanced twins can be utilized to mimic structure execution, improve energy effectiveness, and even anticipate support needs.

The combination of physical and advanced plan is likewise apparent in the field of expanded reality (AR) and computer generated reality (VR). AR overlays advanced data onto the actual world, improving our impression of the climate. VR, then again, submerges clients in completely computerized conditions. Both AR and VR have applications in engineering and configuration, permitting planners and clients to envision and experience spaces before they are fabricated.

The eventual fate of plan and engineering holds energizing prospects, driven by progresses in innovation, materials, and our comprehension of human necessities. Reasonable plan rehearses, informed by natural awareness, will keep on molding the actual scene. In the computerized domain, the combination of man-made consciousness (computer based intelligence) and AI (ML) is ready to reform how programming frameworks are planned, advanced, and customized to client inclinations.

The convergence of plan and innovation is a unique space where development prospers. The reconciliation of sensors, information examination, and simulated intelligence in both physical and advanced plan processes opens new roads for establishing responsive and versatile conditions. Savvy urban communities, for instance, influence innovation to improve metropolitan living, from insightful transportation frameworks to energy-effective structures.

### 3.1 The role of design in creating a welcoming shopping environment

The job of configuration in establishing an inviting shopping climate is a multilayered and vital part of the retail insight. The plan of a retail space incorporates different components, from the format and style to the selection of varieties, lighting, and, surprisingly, the plan of product. This multitude of parts meet up to shape the climate and impact the general view of the shopping climate.

One of the principal contemplations in retail configuration is the design of the store. How items are coordinated and the progression of the space altogether influence the client's excursion. A thoroughly examined design works with simple route, supports investigation, and upgrades the general shopping experience. Contemplations like the position of paths, the plan of item classifications, and the area of high-traffic regions add to establishing a consistent and natural shopping climate.

The style of a retail space assume a significant part in establishing the vibe and making an inviting climate. The plan components, including variety plans, signage, and style, add to the generally speaking visual character of the store. Warm and welcoming tones, decisively positioned lighting, and durable plan topics can bring out good feelings and cause clients to feel great and locked in. Consistency in plan components across the store cultivates a feeling of solidarity and rationality, building up the brand character.

Lighting configuration is a vital part of establishing an inviting shopping climate. Appropriate lighting features items and showcases as well as impacts the temperament and feeling of the space. Normal light, when accessible, is frequently liked for its capacity to make a lovely and bona fide air. Counterfeit lighting, then again, can be utilized decisively to highlight explicit regions, make central focuses, and improve the general perceivability and allure of items.

Notwithstanding visual components, the hear-able climate adds to the general feeling of a retail space. Smart thought of ambient sound or soundscapes can improve the shopping experience. The decision of music ought to line up with the brand character and target segment, making a firm tangible encounter. Furthermore, overseeing encompassing commotion levels is pivotal to guarantee an agreeable and pleasant climate for clients.

The plan of product inside the store is a basic part of retail plan. Item shows shouldn't just be outwardly engaging yet additionally decisively coordinated to work with simple perusing and navigation.

Gathering items by classification, making central focuses with included things, and integrating narrating through showcases can catch the consideration of customers and guide them through an organized shopping venture.

The idea of experiential retail has acquired noticeable quality lately, accentuating the significance of making important and vivid shopping encounters. Configuration assumes a crucial part in creating these encounters, whether through intuitive showcases, tangible components, or extraordinary building highlights. Experiential retail goes past value-based communications, planning to make close to home associations between the brand and the client.

The plan of retail spaces stretches out to the outside, including customer facing facades and passages. An enticing outside makes way for the whole shopping experience. Clear signage, alluring window shows, and very much kept up with veneers add to the underlying feeling clients have of the store. Making a tastefully satisfying and effectively unmistakable retail facade improves the perceivability and allure of the retail space, attracting expected clients.

The job of innovation in retail configuration has extended with the coordination of advanced components. Intuitive showcases, touchscreen interfaces, and expanded reality (AR) applications add to a seriously captivating and dynamic shopping climate. Computerized signage can be utilized to pass on data, grandstand advancements, and give continuous updates. The consistent reconciliation of innovation into the actual retail space upgrades the general client experience and mirrors a contemporary and ground breaking way to deal with plan.

In the period of web based business, the plan of actual retail spaces should develop to offer novel benefits that web based shopping can't reproduce. Personalization is a vital component in this development, where the plan of the store takes special care of the singular inclinations and necessities of clients. From customized proposals in view of procurement history to in-store encounters custom-made to explicit client portions, plan assumes a urgent part in making a feeling of individualized consideration and association.

The idea of maintainability is progressively impacting the plan of retail spaces. Eco-accommodating materials, energy-effective lighting, and naturally cognizant practices are becoming vital to current retail plan. Practical plan lines up with moral and natural contemplations as well as reverberates with earth cognizant purchasers, adding to a positive brand picture.

The job of configuration in establishing an inviting shopping climate is intently attached to the idea of close to home plan. Close to home plan goes past the practical parts of a space and tries to bring out unambiguous feelings and reactions from clients.

This can be accomplished through the cautious choice of varieties, surfaces, and plan components that resound with the interest group. Profound plan makes an association between the client and the brand, cultivating steadfastness and positive affiliations.

Client solace is a vital thought in retail plan. Factors like seating regions, bathrooms, and fitting rooms add to the general comfort and fulfillment of customers. The essential situation of conveniences and the smart plan of spaces for unwinding or connection furnish clients with a more charming and peaceful shopping experience. Consideration regarding these subtleties mirrors a client driven way to deal with plan.

Wayfinding is a basic part of retail configuration, guaranteeing that clients can undoubtedly explore the store and find what they are searching for. Clear signage, natural designs, and decisively positioned data focuses add to viable wayfinding. A very much planned wayfinding framework upgrades the client experience as well as lessens disappointment and improves the probability of clients investigating various region of the store.

In the domain of online retail, the plan of web based business stages is similarly critical in establishing an inviting virtual shopping climate. The UI, visual feel, and in general client experience assume a urgent part in forming the web based shopping venture. Natural route, clear item pictures, and a consistent checkout process add to a positive internet shopping experience, encouraging consumer loyalty and devotion.

The combination of omni-channel techniques further underlines the interconnectedness of physical and advanced retail plan. Clients frequently move flawlessly among on the web and disconnected channels, and a strong plan approach guarantees a steady brand insight across these touchpoints. Whether coming up or on the web, the plan components ought to line up with the brand personality and make a brought together client experience.

All in all, the job of configuration in establishing an inviting shopping climate is an all encompassing and vital undertaking that thinks about a horde of elements. From the format and feel of actual retail spaces to the UI and experience of online stages, plan impacts the manner in which clients see and cooperate with a brand. A very much planned shopping climate goes past simple usefulness, meaning to make important encounters, inspire positive feelings, and cultivate enduring associations between the brand and the client. As retail keeps on developing, the significance of smart and client driven plan stays a foundation of progress in the dynamic and cutthroat scene of the retail business.

**3.2 Notable architectural trends in modern shopping centers**

In the contemporary retail scene, malls have advanced past simple business spaces into dynamic and experiential conditions. Remarkable engineering patterns have arisen, forming the plan and usefulness of present day retail outlets. These patterns mirror the changing inclinations of purchasers, headways in innovation, and a craving to make remarkable and drawing in spaces that go past customary retail.

One unmistakable design pattern in current retail plazas is the mix of blended use spaces. Past being places exclusively for shopping, these focuses now integrate a blend of retail, eating, diversion, and, surprisingly, private parts. The objective is to make energetic and multifunctional objections that take special care of different requirements and inclinations. Blended use improvements upgrade the general insight by offering an extensive and incorporated climate where individuals can reside, work, and play.

Maintainability has turned into a focal concentration in engineering patterns for retail plazas. With an expanded attention to natural issues, engineers and draftsmen are consolidating eco-accommodating plan standards into the preparation and development of these spaces. Green structure materials, energy-effective frameworks, and maintainable practices, for example, water gathering and green rooftops, add to decreasing the ecological effect of malls. Manageability isn't just a mindful decision yet additionally lines up with the inclinations of ecologically cognizant buyers.

Open and breezy plans are supplanting the conventional encased shopping center idea. Draftsmen are embracing open formats that integrate normal light, green spaces, and outside components. This plan pattern expects to make a seriously welcoming and lovely environment, creating some distance from the encased, enormous inclination frequently connected with customary shopping centers. Open plans likewise consider better combination with the encompassing scene, encouraging an association between the retail plaza and the local area.

The idea of experiential retail has significantly affected the engineering plan of present day malls. Purchasers are looking for something beyond a conditional encounter; they want vivid and noteworthy cooperations. Designers are answering by integrating experiential components like intuitive establishments, workmanship establishments, and occasion spaces inside retail outlets. These highlights change the space into an objective where guests can draw in with the climate past shopping, encouraging a feeling of local area and association.

One more design pattern in current retail outlets is the combination of innovation to improve the general insight. Brilliant and associated spaces influence advancements like increased reality (AR), augmented reality (VR), and the Web of Things (IoT) to make intelligent and customized encounters for customers. Computerized signage, touchscreens, and versatile applications give data, wayfinding help, and advancements, adding a layer of intelligence to the actual retail climate.

Adaptable and versatile spaces are turning out to be progressively predominant in the plan of retail plazas. The customary static design is being supplanted by additional dynamic and flexible setups that can oblige various occasions and exercises. Spring up shops, brief establishments, and adaptable occasion spaces take into consideration speedy changes to the retail scene, keeping the mall experience new and locking in.

The plan of current malls likewise mirrors a shift towards neighborhood and local area driven approaches. Designers are integrating components that commend the remarkable personality of the encompassing local area. This can incorporate the utilization of nearby materials, the combination of social themes, and cooperation with neighborhood specialists for public craftsmanship establishments. Local area spaces inside retail outlets, for example, collective social occasion regions and occasion spaces, add to a feeling of spot and association.

The accentuation on health and prosperity is impacting the design patterns in retail plazas. Plans are integrating highlights that advance a solid way of life, for example, wellness focuses, green spaces, and strolling ways. Regular components, including indoor plants and water highlights, add to a quieting and reviving air. The objective is to establish a climate where guests feel a sense of urgency to shop yet in addition to unwind and focus on their prosperity.

In light of the ascent of online business, designers are rethinking the job of actual stores inside retail plazas. The center is moving from value-based spaces to experiential and display area style conditions. Brands are utilizing the actual store as a spot for clients to communicate with items, give them a shot, and draw in with the brand story. This pattern highlights the significance of making extraordinary and paramount in-person encounters that supplement the web based shopping experience.

The idea of savvy and feasible transportation is impacting the plan of current malls. Modelers are consolidating highlights, for example, bicycle paths, electric vehicle charging stations, and productive leaving structures with green rooftops. This mirrors a more extensive pattern towards making harmless to the ecosystem and open spaces that consider the effect of transportation on the general manageability of the retail outlet.

Engineering patterns in current retail plazas likewise remember a concentration for making outwardly striking and notable designs. Engineers are pushing the limits of plan to make structures that act as milestones and add to the personality of the mall. One of a kind exteriors, inventive utilization of materials, and particular building components put these focuses aside, making them unmistakable and paramount.

The mix of workmanship and social components is a developing pattern in the engineering plan of retail outlets. Public craftsmanship establishments, figures, and wall paintings are integrated into the plan to upgrade the stylish allure of the space. Also, malls are becoming settings for far-reaching developments, exhibitions, and presentations. This social coordination not just adds a layer of lavishness to the climate yet in addition cultivates a feeling of local area commitment.

The idea of "retailtainment" is affecting the engineering plan of present day malls. Retail and diversion are flawlessly mixed to make a connecting with and agreeable experience for guests.

This can incorporate the joining of films, gaming zones, live exhibitions, and themed attractions inside the retail outlet. The objective is to expand the length of client visits and make an objective where individuals need to invest energy past shopping.

Draftsmen are progressively focusing on openness and inclusivity in the plan of malls. This includes contemplations, for example, hindrance free plan, widespread openness highlights, and conveniences that take care of people with assorted needs. Making spaces that are inviting and obliging to individuals of any age and capacities adds to a more comprehensive and socially mindful retail climate.

The structural pattern of information driven plan is arising as innovation keeps on assuming an essential part in molding the shopping experience. Information examination and client bits of knowledge are illuminating design choices, from the format of the space to the determination of brands and conveniences. This information driven approach permits planners and designers to establish conditions that are customized to the inclinations and ways of behaving of the interest group, streamlining the general shopping experience.

The fuse of reasonable and nearby materials is an essential pattern in the structural plan of present day retail plazas. From the development stage to the inside wraps up, there is a developing accentuation on utilizing materials that have a negligible natural effect and add to a feeling of legitimacy. This lines up with the more extensive development towards supportable and capable practices in the retail business.

All in all, the design patterns in present day malls mirror a dynamic and developing way to deal with establishing retail conditions. From the combination of blended use spaces to an emphasis on maintainability, innovation, and experiential plan, draftsmen are pushing the limits to live up to the changing assumptions of buyers. The cutting edge mall is presently not simply a spot for exchanges; an objective offers a thorough and drawing in experience, cultivating a feeling of local area and association in the consistently developing retail scene.

### 3.3 Successful and innovative designs

Effective and imaginative plans are the consequence of a blend of inventiveness, usefulness, and a profound comprehension of client needs. Across different fields, from engineering and item plan to advanced connection points and marking, effective plans charm crowds, tackle issues, and frequently rethink the norms inside their particular enterprises. Inspecting key instances of fruitful and imaginative plans gives bits of knowledge into the standards and approaches that add to their adequacy.

In the domain of engineering, the Sydney Drama House remains as a notable and imaginative plan. Planned by the Danish draftsman Jørn Utzon, the Sydney Drama

House is a magnum opus of present day design and an image of Australia. Finished in 1973, its particular shell-like designs are a wonder of designing and style.

The plan epitomizes development in structure, as the modeler drew motivation from normal components, for example, palm leaves and the portions of an orange, to make the special shell structures. The Sydney Show House not just fills in as an incredibly famous social setting yet additionally as a demonstration of the force of earth shattering structural plan.

Another compositional victory that exhibits advancement is the Burj Khalifa in Dubai. Planned by the engineering firm Skidmore, Owings and Merrill, the Burj Khalifa remains as the tallest structure on the planet. Its smooth and tightened plan not just gives a striking visual presence on the Dubai horizon yet additionally addresses reasonable contemplations, like breeze opposition and underlying dependability. The Burj Khalifa's inventive plan stretches out to its maintainable elements, including a framework that gathers buildup from the structure's cooling framework to inundate close by green spaces. This blend of tasteful allure, designing development, and supportability makes the Burj Khalifa a champion illustration of fruitful plan in the domain of engineering.

Moving into the space of item plan, the Apple iPhone has turned into a worldview of development and achievement. Sent off in 2007, the iPhone changed the cell phone industry with its touchscreen interface, moderate plan, and consistent reconciliation of equipment and programming. The iPhone's prosperity lies in its mechanical progressions as well as in its client driven plan reasoning. Apple's emphasis on making a gadget that is natural, tastefully satisfying, and easy to use has set a norm for the whole purchaser hardware industry. The constant advancement of the iPhone, with every cycle presenting new elements and upgrades, represents the organization's obligation to development and client experience.

In the auto business, the Tesla Model S addresses a forward leap in electric vehicle plan. Sent off in 2012, the Model S re-imagined impression of electric vehicles by offering a smooth and elite exhibition option in contrast to conventional fuel controlled vehicles. Its creative plan incorporates an open and moderate inside with a huge touchscreen control board, unmistakable bird of prey wing entryways in the Model X variation, and the fuse of state of the art independent driving highlights. The outcome of the Tesla Model S has moved the reception of electric vehicles as well as provoked laid out automakers to reevaluate their plan and innovation methodologies.

In the domain of computerized plan, the UI (UI) and client experience (UX) plan of the Airbnb stage play had a critical impact in the organization's prosperity. Airbnb upset the neighborliness business by giving a stage that permits people to lease their homes or properties to voyagers. The site and portable application highlight an instinctive and outwardly engaging connection point that improves on the most common way of finding and booking facilities. The utilization of excellent visuals, a clear reserving framework, and customized suggestions add to a positive client

# SHOPPING CENTERS UNVEILED

experience. Airbnb's creative plan has upset the customary lodging industry as well as impacted the more extensive sharing economy.

The progress of online entertainment stages is frequently attached to their UIs, and Instagram stands apart as a great representation. Sent off in 2010, Instagram immediately acquired notoriety for its emphasis on visual substance and easy to understand plan. The straightforwardness of its connection point, based on photograph and video sharing, added to its quick reception. The presentation of elements, for example, channels and Stories further upgraded the stage's allure. Instagram's plan decisions, stressing visual narrating and usability, assumed a vital part in its development and supported progress in the serious web-based entertainment scene.

In the field of visual depiction and marking, the Coca-Cola logo remains as quite possibly of the most conspicuous and getting through plan on the planet. Made by Forthright Bricklayer Robinson in 1885, the content textual style and red-and-white variety plan of the Coca-Cola logo have become inseparable from the brand. The plan's prosperity lies in its effortlessness, memorability, and agelessness. Notwithstanding various updates and upgrades in the publicizing business throughout the long term, the center components of the Coca-Cola logo have remained generally unaltered, showing the persevering through force of a very much created and famous plan.

The Nike Swoosh logo is one more illustration of effective marking and visual communication. Made by visual depiction understudy Carolyn Davidson in 1971, the Swoosh has turned into a universally perceived image of the Nike brand. Its effortlessness and dynamic shape convey a feeling of development and speed, adjusting impeccably with Nike's way of life as an athletic apparel and athletic footwear organization. The outcome of the Nike Swoosh lies in its capacity to encapsulate the brand's qualities and resound with purchasers across assorted societies and socioeconomics.

In the domain of modern plan, the Dyson vacuum cleaner is a striking illustration of development. Sir James Dyson, an English designer, changed the vacuum cleaner industry with the presentation of the Dyson bagless vacuum in the late twentieth hundred years. The plan supplanted customary vacuum packs with a cyclonic partition framework, wiping out the requirement for dispensable sacks and further developing pull proficiency. Dyson's obligation to development and client driven plan has extended past vacuum cleaners to incorporate a scope of home devices, all described by smooth feel and state of the art innovation.

The Home Learning Indoor regulator addresses an extraordinary plan in the domain of home innovation. Made by Tony Fadell, one of the personalities behind the iPod, the Home indoor regulator presented a savvy and instinctive way to deal with home environment control. The indoor regulator learns clients' inclinations and changes the temperature in like manner, advancing energy effectiveness and cost reserve funds.

Its smooth round plan, instinctive point of interaction, and network to cell phones epitomize the combination of innovation and client focused plan. The progress of the Home indoor regulator has affected the more extensive market for brilliant home gadgets and has prodded advancements in the field of home computerization.

In the domain of maintainable plan, the One Focal Park improvement in Sydney, Australia, remains as a spearheading model. Planned by planner Jean Nouvel and scene designer Patrick Blanc, One Focal Park highlights two private pinnacles with an interesting reconciliation of vegetation and practical innovations. The pinnacles are decorated with vertical nurseries, and a cantilevered sky garden interfaces the two structures. The imaginative plan consolidates energy-proficient frameworks, water gathering, and a tri-age plant that produces power, warming, and cooling. One Focal Park shows the way that manageable engineering can be stylishly satisfying and add to the prosperity of the two inhabitants and the climate.

The High Line in New York City addresses an extraordinary way to deal with metropolitan plan and scene design. Based on a previous raised railroad track, the High Line is a recreational area that breezes through the Chelsea area. Planned via scene modelers James Corner Field Activities and designers Diller Scofidio + Renfro, the High Line flawlessly coordinates green spaces, strolling ways, and public craftsmanship into the metropolitan texture. The versatile reuse of the railroad track exhibits the potential for reusing existing framework to make inventive and welcoming public spaces.

The Oculus in Lower Manhattan, planned by modeler Santiago Calatrava, is a structural wonder that fills in as the highlight of the World Exchange Community Transportation Center point. The Oculus is a transportation center and mall with a plan enlivened by the picture of a pigeon let out of a youngster's hands. The taking off, wing-like design makes a feeling of transparency and daintiness, representing trust and resurrection. The Oculus shows the way that design can go past simple usefulness to encapsulate strong representative implications and add to the close to home and social texture of a city.

In the advanced domain, the plan of the Tesla Model 3's UI stands apart as an imaginative and easy to use insight. The moderate dashboard includes an enormous touchscreen that controls the greater part of the vehicle's capabilities. The point of interaction is instinctive, responsive, and persistently refreshed through over-the-air programming refreshes. The Tesla Model 3's computerized plan improves on the driving experience as well as addresses a takeoff from conventional auto interfaces, setting new norms for in-vehicle innovation.

The plan of the SpaceX Winged serpent shuttle addresses an earth shattering way to deal with aviation plan. Planned by SpaceX, the Winged serpent shuttle consolidates usefulness with a smooth and modern stylish.

The space apparatus' inside focuses on ease of use and wellbeing for space travelers, while the outside plan consolidates streamlined and primary contemplations. The progress of the Mythical serpent space apparatus configuration adds to the more extensive objectives of making space travel more available and financially savvy.

# SHOPPING CENTERS UNVEILED

In the domain of computer generated reality (VR) and expanded reality (AR), the plan of the Oculus Fracture VR headset plays had a vital impact in promoting vivid encounters. Planned by Oculus VR, an auxiliary of Meta Stages (previously Facebook), the Oculus Crack presented an agreeable and easy to understand VR headset that gives a top notch computer generated simulation experience. Its plan incorporates elements like customizable ties, ergonomic controls, and high-goal shows. The progress of the Oculus Fracture has impacted the more extensive reception of VR innovation for gaming, reenactments, and different applications past amusement.

The Microsoft HoloLens addresses an imaginative plan in the domain of expanded reality. Planned by Microsoft, the HoloLens is a blended reality headset that overlays holographic pictures onto the client's actual climate. Its plan integrates sensors, cameras, and high level optics to flawlessly mix computerized and actual real factors. The HoloLens has applications in fields like medical services, schooling, and modern plan, displaying the capability of expanded reality to upgrade certifiable encounters.

In the field of style plan, the Nike Flyknit innovation addresses a progressive way to deal with athletic shoe plan. The Flyknit innovation, presented in 2012, includes utilizing a solitary strand of yarn to weave the whole upper piece of a shoe, giving a lightweight and perfectly sized plan. This creative methodology decreases squander as well as improves the general solace and execution of athletic footwear. Nike's Flyknit innovation has since been generally taken on in the athletic shoe industry, representing the effect of imaginative materials and assembling methods on plan.

The Aeron Seat by Herman Mill operator is a milestone illustration of ergonomic office seat plan. Presented in 1994 and planned by Bill Stumpf and Wear Chadwick, the Aeron Seat includes a momentous plan that focuses on solace, backing, and flexibility. The seat's lattice material gives a harmony between help and breathability, while its inventive changes oblige an extensive variety of body types and sitting inclinations. The Aeron Seat has turned into a famous piece of office furniture and an image of the significance of ergonomic plan in making agreeable and useful work areas.

The outcome of these creative plans across different fields originates from a mix of elements that add to their usefulness, feel, and client experience. Consistent ideas among these plans incorporate a profound comprehension of client needs, a promise to pushing the limits of customary reasoning, and an emphasis on coordinating innovation to improve execution and ease of use.

Whether in engineering, item plan, computerized interfaces, or different disciplines, fruitful and imaginative plans frequently share a devotion to taking care of certifiable issues, making essential encounters, and leaving an enduring effect on their separate businesses.

Development in plan is a dynamic and consistently developing cycle that includes pushing the limits of imagination, usefulness, and client experience. Across different fields, from engineering and item plan to advanced connection points and transportation, creative plans have the ability to change enterprises, tackle complex issues, and reclassify the manner in which we communicate with the world. Looking at key instances of creative plans gives bits of knowledge into the standards and approaches that add to their prosperity.

One of the famous instances of imaginative engineering configuration is the Guggenheim Historical center in Bilbao, Spain, planned by designer Honest Gehry. Finished in 1997, the Guggenheim Bilbao is famous for its deconstructivist design, portrayed by natural structures, bended volumes, and whimsical utilization of materials like titanium and glass. The historical center's plan difficulties customary thoughts of gallery design as well as changes the metropolitan scene of Bilbao. Gehry's creative way to deal with structure and materials has made the Guggenheim Bilbao a social milestone and an image of engineering development.

The Eden Task in Cornwall, Joined Realm, is one more building wonder that epitomizes development in plan. Planned by Sir Nicholas Grimshaw and opened in 2001, the Eden Undertaking comprises of a progression of enormous geodesic vaults, known as biomes, lodging various environments. The biomes are developed from hexagonal and pentagonal expanded plastic cells, making a lightweight yet durable design. The creative plan permits the Eden Venture to work as a worldwide nursery, exhibiting different plant species in controlled conditions. This way to deal with manageable engineering shows the way that inventive plan can address ecological difficulties and make vivid instructive encounters.

In the domain of item plan, the Tesla Powerwall addresses a weighty development in energy capacity. Presented by Tesla in 2015, the Powerwall is a battery-powered lithium-particle battery intended for private use. Its smooth and conservative plan permits it to be mounted on a wall, and it flawlessly coordinates with sun powered chargers to store overabundance energy for sometime in the future. The Powerwall embodies the crossing point of innovation and supportability, giving property holders a way to saddle and store environmentally friendly power for expanded independence.

The Home Learning Indoor regulator, planned by Tony Fadell and presented in 2011, is one more illustration of creative item plan. The Home indoor regulator altered the home environment control industry by consolidating AI calculations to adjust to clients' inclinations after some time.

Its instinctive connection point, moderate plan, and capacity to be controlled somewhat through cell phones have set new guidelines for indoor regulator plan. The Home Learning Indoor regulator upgrades energy effectiveness as well as shows the way that insightful plan can change regular family objects into clever and easy to use gadgets.

In the car business, the Tesla Model S stands apart as an exploring plan that joins electric power with elite execution. Sent off in 2012, the Model S tested ordinary thoughts of electric vehicles by offering a smooth and lavish plan combined with noteworthy reach and speed increase. Its moderate inside, overwhelmed by an enormous touchscreen control board, epitomizes Tesla's obligation to inventive plan and state of the art innovation. The progress of the Model S plays had a critical impact in reshaping the view of electric vehicles and speeding up the change to economical transportation.

The BMW i3, presented in 2013, is one more vital illustration of advancement in auto plan. As an electric city vehicle, the BMW i3 highlights an unmistakable outside made of lightweight carbon fiber-built up plastic, adding to its energy proficiency and reach. The inside plan underscores manageability with the utilization of reused and sustainable materials. The BMW i3 exhibits how inventive plan can be consistently coordinated with natural cognizance to make a ground breaking and effective metropolitan versatility arrangement.

In the domain of computerized plan, the iPhone, presented by Mac in 2007, remains as an extraordinary development that reformed the cell phone industry. Planned by Jonathan Ive, the iPhone consolidated a smooth and moderate stylish with a pivotal touch interface. Its mix of equipment and programming, instinctive UI, and the Application Store environment re-imagined the manner in which individuals associate with cell phones. The iPhone's prosperity significantly affects the whole customer hardware industry, setting new norms for plan, usefulness, and client experience.

The Tesla Model 3's UI addresses one more outstanding illustration of development in advanced plan. Sent off in 2017, the Model 3 highlights a moderate dashboard with a solitary focal touchscreen that controls most vehicle capabilities. The connection point is persistently refreshed through over-the-air programming refreshes, exhibiting Tesla's obligation to giving clients new highlights and enhancements. The Model 3's computerized plan works on the driving experience as well as mirrors a takeoff from customary car interfaces, embracing a more present day and associated approach.

In the domain of UIs and encounters, the plan of the Airbnb stage plays had an essential impact in disturbing the conventional friendliness industry. Sent off in 2008, Airbnb's site and portable application highlight a natural and outwardly engaging connection point that works on the most common way of finding and booking facilities.

The utilization of great visuals, a direct reserving framework, and customized proposals add to a positive client experience. Airbnb's imaginative plan has not just changed the manner in which individuals travel and track down housing yet has likewise affected the more extensive sharing economy.

The visual communication and marking of organizations like Apple and Nike embody the force of imaginative visual correspondence. Apple's image personality, portrayed by clean lines, straightforwardness, and an emphasis on the item, has become inseparable from development and premium quality. The notable Apple logo, planned by Ransack Janoff in 1977, stays an immortal and conspicuous image. Nike's Swoosh logo, made by visual communication understudy Carolyn Davidson in 1971, conveys a feeling of development and speed, adjusting impeccably with the brand's way of life as an active apparel and athletic footwear organization. Both Apple and

Nike grandstand how successful visual plan can lift a brand and make serious areas of strength for an association with shoppers.

In the field of modern plan, the Dyson Airblade hand dryer addresses a creative answer for a typical issue. Planned by Sir James Dyson and presented in 2006, the Airblade utilizes fast sheets of unheated air to dry hands rapidly and productively. Its plan takes out the requirement for paper towels or conventional hand dryers, adding to ecological supportability. The Airblade's smooth and smaller plan represents how advancement in modern plan can further develop usefulness, decrease waste, and improve client experience.

The Google Pixel Buds, presented in 2017, feature advancement in the plan of remote headphones. The Pixel Buds include a conservative and ergonomic plan, giving a solid fit and open to listening experience. One of the champion highlights is continuous language interpretation, permitting clients to have discussions in various dialects. The Pixel Buds show the way that plan development can stretch out past feel to incorporate elements that improve usefulness and reclassify the capacities of regular embellishments.

In the domain of economical plan, the Sun oriented Motivation 2 is a notable illustration of development in flight. Planned by Bertrand Piccard and André Borschberg, the Sun oriented Drive 2 is a sun based controlled airplane that finished a noteworthy around-the-world trip in 2016. The airplane's wings are outfitted with sunlight based chargers that create energy to control its electric engines. The Sun based Motivation 2 represents how creative plan and innovation can be saddled to accomplish supportable and eco-accommodating arrangements in the transportation business.

In the domain of metropolitan plan and engineering, the High Line in New York City addresses an imaginative way to deal with reusing metropolitan framework. Planned by James Corner Field Tasks and Diller Scofidio + Renfro, the High Line is a recreational area based on a previous raised rail route track.

The plan flawlessly incorporates green spaces, strolling ways, and public workmanship into the metropolitan texture, making an extraordinary and connecting with public space. The outcome of the Great Line has enlivened comparative undertakings around the world, showing the way that smart metropolitan plan can change neglected spaces into lively and local area driven conditions.

The Warka Water Pinnacle, planned by Arturo Vittori and presented in 2015, addresses an imaginative answer for tending to water shortage in rustic regions. The pinnacle, propelled by regular components like termite hills and the state of leaves, gathers and consolidates water from the air utilizing a lattice structure. The Warka Water Pinnacle shows the way that imaginative plan can add to tackling squeezing worldwide difficulties by giving admittance to perfect and economical water sources.

In the domain of style plan, the adidas Futurecraft 4D shoe exhibits development in both plan and assembling. Presented in 2018, the Futurecraft 4D elements a padded sole made through computerized light blend, a cycle that utilizations light and oxygen to shape fluid sap into a responsive and adjustable cross section structure. The shoe's plan focuses on execution and solace as well as represents the capability of cutting edge fabricating advancements in the style business. The Futurecraft 4D represents how development in materials and creation strategies can reclassify the potential outcomes of footwear plan.

The Nike Flyknit innovation addresses a groundbreaking way to deal with athletic shoe plan. Presented in 2012, Flyknit includes utilizing a solitary strand of yarn to sew the whole upper piece of a shoe, giving a lightweight and perfectly sized plan. This creative methodology decreases squander as well as upgrades the general solace and execution of athletic footwear. Nike's Flyknit innovation has since been broadly taken on in the athletic shoe industry, outlining the effect of creative materials and assembling strategies on plan.

In the domain of transportation plan, the Hyperloop idea, proposed by Elon Musk in 2013, addresses a visionary way to deal with high velocity transportation. The Hyperloop imagines traveler units going through low-pressure tubes at very high rates, lessening travel time between urban communities. Albeit the Hyperloop is still in the applied stage, its creative plan has started revenue and interest chasing after quicker and more productive transportation arrangements.

The progress of these inventive plans across different fields can be credited to a mix of elements that add to their viability and effect. Consistent ideas among these plans incorporate a profound comprehension of client needs, a pledge to pushing the limits of traditional reasoning, and an emphasis on coordinating innovation to improve execution and ease of use. Whether in engineering, item plan, computerized interfaces, or different disciplines, imaginative plans frequently share a devotion to taking care of genuine issues, making significant encounters, and leaving an enduring effect on their particular businesses.

# Chapter 4

**Tenant Mix and Leasing Strategies**

Occupant blend and renting systems are basic parts in the outcome of any business land improvement. The cautious choice of occupants and the execution of powerful renting procedures can essentially influence the general exhibition and productivity of a property. In this thorough investigation, we will dig into the critical parts of occupant blend and renting methodologies, looking at their significance, best practices, and the advancing patterns in the unique universe of business land.

At the center of a fruitful inhabitant blend is a profound comprehension of the objective market and the particular requirements and inclinations of the encompassing local area. The cycle starts with intensive statistical surveying to distinguish the socioeconomics, psychographics, and spending examples of the neighborhood populace. By acquiring bits of knowledge into the local area's qualities, engineers and land owners can fit their inhabitant blend to fulfill the need for labor and products, at last upgrading the property's allure for the two buyers and planned occupants.

The retail scene has gone through huge changes as of late, determined by changes in shopper conduct and mechanical headways. Online business has arisen as an imposing power, testing customary physical retail. Therefore, effective inhabitant blend methodologies should adjust to these movements, consolidating a blend of on the web and disconnected retailers to make a strong and versatile retail biological system.

Finding some kind of harmony between anchor inhabitants and specialty retailers is a pivotal part of occupant blend arranging. Anchor inhabitants, regularly enormous, deep rooted retailers, draw huge people walking through and act as key attractions for a business property. These anchors add to the general imperativeness of the turn of events and assume a vital part in molding the impression of the space. Nonetheless, a balanced inhabitant blend goes past anchors, incorporating a different exhibit of specialty retailers that take care of specialty markets and deal interesting items or administrations.

Notwithstanding retail, the inhabitant blend reaches out to different areas, like feasting, amusement, and administrations. Counting a blend of experiential contributions, like cafés, films, and wellness focuses, can make an objective that goes past simple shopping. This expansion upgrades the general insight for guests and urges them to invest more energy in the vicinity, cultivating a feeling of local area and commitment.

Renting techniques assume a crucial part in molding the occupant blend and boosting the worth of a business property. The renting system includes a progression of basic strides, from drawing in and tying down occupants to arranging lease terms and cultivating continuous connections. A successful renting procedure isn't just about occupying empty spaces yet additionally about adjusting inhabitant profiles to the general vision for the property.

One critical thought in renting systems is the exchange of rent terms. Rent arrangements are complicated reports that frame the freedoms as well as expectations of the two landowners and inhabitants. The exchange cycle includes conversations on rental rates, rent span, inhabitant enhancements, and different terms that can altogether influence the monetary exhibition of the property. Striking a fair and commonly gainful arrangement requires a profound comprehension of economic situations, the serious scene, and the particular necessities of the two players.

In a quickly developing business sector, adaptability in renting plans has become progressively significant. More limited rent terms, rent reestablishments, and choices for extension or compression give occupants the dexterity to adjust to changing business conditions. Landowners, thusly, benefit from the possibility to change rental rates in light of market vacillations and the capacity to draw in and hold occupants in a profoundly serious climate.

Occupant improvement stipends (TIAs) are a typical part of renting exchanges, especially in the retail and office areas. TIAs are reserves allotted via property managers to improve or alter the rented space as per the occupant's requirements.

This can incorporate inside form outs, redesigns, and the establishment of specific gear. The discussion of TIAs requires cautious thought of the extent of enhancements, cost-sharing plans, and the effect on the property's general worth.

The execution of compelling advertising and special techniques is one more key component in renting achievement. Making mindfulness about the property and its occupants is fundamental for drawing in the two shoppers and likely occupants. In the present computerized age, web based promoting, virtual entertainment, and designated publicizing assume an essential part in arriving at the interest group and building a positive impression of the property.

Cooperation with inhabitants on joint advertising drives can additionally improve the perceivability of the property. Composed special occasions, devotion projects, and cross-advancements among inhabitants can make a synergistic impact, driving expanded people walking through and cultivating a feeling of local area inside the business space.

The renting system is definitely not a one-time exchange however a continuous connection among property managers and inhabitants. Constructing and keeping up areas of strength for with connections add to inhabitant maintenance, diminishing opportunity rates and the related expenses of turnover. Normal correspondence, responsiveness to occupant needs, and proactive property the board are fundamental parts of a fruitful inhabitant relationship the executives technique.

Notwithstanding conventional renting models, arising patterns in the business land industry are forming new ways to deal with occupant blend and renting techniques. The ascent of spring up stores, transient leases, and adaptable spaces mirrors the developing idea of purchaser inclinations and the requirement for versatility even with quick changes on the lookout.

Spring up stores, specifically, have acquired fame for of making novel and connecting retail encounters. These impermanent retail spaces permit brands to test new business sectors, produce buzz, and associate with shoppers in creative ways. Property managers can use the pattern of spring up stores by integrating adaptable renting plans that oblige transient occupants, giving a dynamic and steadily changing climate for guests.

The idea of adaptable work areas has likewise affected renting methodologies, particularly in the workplace area. Cooperating spaces and adaptable office suppliers offer organizations the capacity to increase their tasks or down in view of their nearby requirements. Landowners can take advantage of this pattern by integrating adaptable office spaces inside their properties, taking special care of the developing interest for deft and versatile workplaces.

Innovation assumes an essential part in current occupant blend and renting techniques. The utilization of information examination, computerized reasoning, and progressed renting programming empowers landowners and property administrators to go with informed choices, streamline renting cycles, and upgrade generally functional proficiency.

Information examination give significant bits of knowledge into buyer conduct, permitting land owners to recognize patterns, inclinations, and regions for development. This information driven approach stretches out to occupant determination, assisting property managers with picking inhabitants that line up with the inclinations and requirements of the objective market. Progressed investigation additionally add to more precise anticipating of renting patterns, empowering proactive direction and vital preparation.

Man-made reasoning (man-made intelligence) is progressively being used in renting cycles to robotize routine errands, smooth out work processes, and improve the general productivity of property the executives. Computer based intelligence driven instruments can dissect huge datasets, distinguish designs, and produce significant experiences, saving time for property supervisors to zero in on essential direction and occupant relationship the executives.

Renting programming stages offer exhaustive answers for dealing with the whole renting lifecycle. From prospecting and lead the executives to rent organization and detailing, these stages concentrate data, further develop correspondence, and work with joint effort between landowners, inhabitants, and different partners. The reception of renting programming adds to a more straightforward and smoothed out renting process, decreasing managerial weights and limiting the gamble of blunders.

As manageability turns into an undeniably significant thought in land improvement, green renting has arisen as a pattern that adjusts ecological, social, and monetary goals. Green renting includes integrating maintainable practices into rent arrangements, with an emphasis on energy effectiveness, squander decrease, and earth capable structure rehearses.

Landowners and occupants can work together on drives, for example, energy-productive structure configuration, water protection measures, and waste decrease programs. Green leases might incorporate arrangements for harmless to the ecosystem building affirmations, like LEED (Authority in Energy and Ecological Plan), and lay out shared supportability objectives that benefit the two players.

The execution of green renting adds to natural stewardship as well as lines up with the inclinations of an undeniably eco-cognizant buyer base. Reasonable practices can improve the attractiveness of a property, draw in earth disapproved of occupants, and position the improvement as a dependable and ground breaking resource locally.

All in all, occupant blend and renting techniques are vital parts in the progress of business land advancements. The cautious curation of a different and reciprocal occupant blend, combined with compelling renting procedures, can upgrade the general engaging quality, productivity, and manageability of a property.

Exhaustive statistical surveying, a comprehension of shopper conduct, and flexibility to arising patterns are fundamental components in making an occupant blend that reverberates with the neighborhood local area. The renting system, from exchange to progressing relationship the board, requires a key and cooperative methodology that thinks about the necessities of the two landowners and occupants.

The unique idea of the business land scene requests adaptability and advancement in renting methodologies. The fuse of transient leases, spring up stores, and adaptable work areas mirrors the advancing inclinations of purchasers and organizations. Innovation, including information investigation, computerized reasoning, and renting programming, engages land owners to settle on informed choices and smooth out renting processes.

As manageability turns into a focal thought, green renting rehearses offer a chance for landowners and occupants to team up on earth mindful drives. By lining up with maintainable practices, properties can engage a more extensive crowd, add to ecological preservation, and position themselves as pioneers in capable land improvement.

In the consistently impacting universe of business land, achievement lies in the capacity to adjust, advance, and develop dynamic occupant blend and renting methodologies that reverberate with the developing requirements of both the market and the local area. By embracing these standards, land owners and engineers can situate their resources for long haul outcome in a cutthroat and dynamic industry.

### 4.1 Importance of a diverse tenant mix

The significance of a different occupant blend in business land couldn't possibly be more significant. A well-organized and different cluster of occupants contributes fundamentally to the general achievement, dynamic quality, and versatility of a property. In this investigation, we will dig into the complex justifications for why a different occupant blend is significant, looking at the financial, social, and key advantages that emerge from the purposeful consideration of various inhabitants inside a business improvement.

At its center, a different occupant blend is a financial goal. By offering a scope of labor and products, a property can draw in an expansive segment, guaranteeing that it stays pertinent and interesting to a wide cross-part of the nearby populace. This monetary variety is especially significant in relieving gambles related with changes in shopper inclinations, financial slumps, or industry-explicit difficulties that might influence individual occupants.

In the midst of financial vulnerability, having a different occupant blend goes about as a defend for land owners and property managers. A dependence on a solitary industry or sort of occupant makes a property defenseless against the promising and less promising times of that specific area. Then again, an enhanced occupant blend spreads risk, making the property stronger to monetary shocks. This hazard moderation procedure is particularly appropriate in the result of worldwide occasions, for example, financial downturns or general wellbeing emergencies, where certain ventures might be excessively affected.

Past monetary contemplations, a different inhabitant blend adds to the social texture of a local area. Business improvements are not simply actual spaces; they are social center points that shape the personality and character of an area. At the point when a property has various inhabitants, including retail shops, eateries, social spaces, and local area administrations, it turns into an objective that draws in individuals from various different backgrounds.

This social variety establishes a dynamic and comprehensive climate, encouraging a feeling of local area and network. A property with a different inhabitant blend turns into a social occasion place where individuals can interface, share encounters, and add to the making of a dynamic and drawing in nearby culture. The social part of different occupant blend goes past the conditional idea of business spaces, changing them into local area resources that upgrade the general personal satisfaction in the encompassing region.

Notwithstanding monetary and social advantages, a different occupant blend improves the general engaging quality and attractiveness of a property. At the point when likely inhabitants or financial backers assess a business improvement, they think about the scope of contributions and the collaboration among occupants. A property with a different blend is bound to stick out and interest a more extensive crowd.

The different occupant blend makes a positive input circle. As additional individuals are attracted to the property for its shifted contributions, it turns into an undeniably appealing objective for organizations looking to rent space. This elevated attractiveness can prompt expanded interest for rental space, possibly permitting property managers to order higher rental rates and giving an upper hand on the lookout.

Decisively, a different occupant blend permits land owners to gain by arising patterns and changes in shopper conduct. Markets are dynamic, and inclinations advance after some time. By having a blend of inhabitants that take care of various necessities and inclinations, a property can adjust all the more successfully to moving purchaser requests.

For instance, the ascent of online business has changed the retail scene, prompting the conclusion of numerous customary physical stores. Be that as it may, properties with a different occupant blend can explore these progressions all the more effectively.

While certain retailers might confront difficulties, others, for example, experiential or administration situated organizations, may flourish. This flexibility to showcase patterns positions a property for long haul manageability and achievement.

Moreover, a different occupant blend encourages development and inventiveness inside a business improvement. At the point when organizations from various businesses coincide in a similar space, there is a characteristic trade of thoughts and cross-fertilization of imagination. This cooperative energy can prompt cooperative drives, joint showcasing endeavors, and inventive plans of action that benefit the two inhabitants and the general property.

In the domain of retail, for example, a different blend could incorporate laid out anchor occupants close by arising shop stockpiles spring up shops. This blend makes a shopping experience that takes special care of a large number of inclinations, from those looking for notable brands to those searching for interesting and specialty contributions. The transaction among laid out and arising organizations creates a unique environment that keeps the property new and locking in.

The different occupant blend isn't restricted to retail however stretches out to different areas like eating, amusement, and administrations. The consideration of different feasting choices, including ethnic foods and specialty cafés, can change a property into a culinary objective. Diversion contributions, like films, live execution settings, or sporting spaces, add to the property's general allure as a spot for relaxation and mingling.

In the workplace area, a different occupant blend might incorporate a blend of corporate workplaces, cooperating spaces, and innovation new companies. This blend takes special care of the shifted needs of organizations, from laid out ventures requiring customary office spaces to dynamic new businesses looking for adaptable and cooperative workplaces. The cooperative energy between various sorts of office inhabitants can make a rich environment that cultivates organizing, information trade, and business development.

The significance of a different occupant blend is especially clear in blended use improvements, where private, business, and sporting spaces exist together. The mix of private parts adds one more layer of variety, acquiring inhabitants with various ways of life, socioeconomics, and inclinations. This private variety supplements the business blend, establishing a comprehensive and comprehensive climate where individuals can reside, work, and associate inside a similar local area.

While the advantages of a different occupant blend are obvious, accomplishing and keeping up with such variety requires deliberate preparation and continuous administration. Land owners and engineers should cautiously organize the occupant blend, considering the particular necessities of the nearby market, the property's situating, and the all-encompassing vision for the turn of events.

Statistical surveying assumes a critical part in grasping the socioeconomics, inclinations, and buying force of the main interest group. This information driven approach advises choices about the sorts regarding occupants that would resound with the neighborhood local area and add to the general variety of the property.

In the renting system, property managers ought to effectively look for a blend of anchor occupants, specialty retailers, and specialist organizations that complete one another. The exchange of rent terms, including rental rates, rent length, and occupant improvement remittances, requires an offset that lines up with the monetary objectives of the two property managers and inhabitants.

Besides, continuous administration and commitment with inhabitants are fundamental for keeping a different occupant blend. Landowners ought to cultivate a climate that empowers joint effort and correspondence among occupants. Facilitated promoting endeavors, joint occasions, and shared drives can improve the general allure of the property and make a feeling of union among the different cluster of organizations.

The administration of a different occupant blend likewise includes tending to possible struggles and guaranteeing that the requirements of all inhabitants are met. Fair and straightforward strategies, powerful question goal components, and proactive property the executives add to a positive and agreeable climate that energizes inhabitant maintenance.

All in all, the significance of a different occupant blend in business land reaches out across monetary, social, and vital aspects. A well-organized blend of occupants adds to the monetary strength of a property, moderating dangers related with market variances and financial slumps. The social variety made by a blend of retail, feasting, diversion, and administration inhabitants changes business improvements into dynamic local area center points that upgrade the general personal satisfaction.

Decisively, a different inhabitant blend positions a property to adjust to changing business sector patterns and shopper inclinations. It encourages development, innovativeness, and cooperation among organizations, establishing a unique climate that draws in the two occupants and shoppers. Accomplishing and keeping a different occupant blend requires purposeful preparation, statistical surveying, and progressing the board to guarantee an offset that lines up with the necessities of the nearby local area and the overall vision for the turn of events.

As the business land scene keeps on developing, properties with a different occupant blend are ready to flourish, giving financial accomplishment to property managers as well as adding to the social and social dynamic quality of the networks they serve.

### 4.2 Strategies for attracting and retaining tenants

Creating viable systems for drawing in and holding occupants is a basic part of fruitful property the executives in the dynamic and serious scene of business land. Land owners and property managers must proactively address the advancing requirements and inclinations of inhabitants while establishing a climate that encourages long haul connections. In this complete investigation, we will dig into different procedures pointed toward drawing in excellent occupants, boosting occupant fulfillment, and at last guaranteeing inhabitant maintenance.

**Grasping Inhabitant Needs and Inclinations**

At the center of any effective inhabitant fascination and maintenance methodology is a profound comprehension of occupant needs and inclinations. Land owners should put time and assets in statistical surveying to acquire bits of knowledge into the particular prerequisites of their objective segment. This includes examining neighborhood market patterns, concentrating on the cutthroat scene, and distinguishing the interesting selling focuses that can separate a property.

Understanding inhabitant needs goes past the actual space. While perspectives like area, size, and conveniences are significant, there is a rising accentuation on making a general encounter that lines up with the way of life and upsides of the objective occupant segment. This could incorporate contemplations, for example, maintainability drives, local area commitment programs, or the combination of innovation inside the property.

**Adaptable and Inventive Renting Designs**

In light of changing business elements and the developing idea of work, land owners are progressively embracing adaptable and creative renting structures. Customary long haul leases are being enhanced with choices for more limited rent terms, collaborating spaces, and versatile office arrangements. This adaptability permits organizations to adjust their land needs with their functional prerequisites, giving a degree of deftness that is especially significant in the present high speed business climate.

Adaptable renting designs can likewise include inventive game plans, for example, income offering arrangements or associations to inhabitants. These models attach the outcome of the occupant's business to the general presentation of the property, encouraging a feeling of joint effort and shared achievement.

**Serious Valuing and Impetuses**

The monetary part of renting is a vital thought for the two occupants and land owners. Offering serious estimating designs and motivators can be a strong technique for drawing in and holding occupants. This could include giving great rental rates, particularly for long haul rents, or offering motivations, for example, lease reductions, occupant improvement recompenses, or adaptable installment terms.

In exceptionally aggressive business sectors, land owners might investigate creative estimating models that line up with the worth gave to occupants. This could incorporate execution based lease, where the rental rate is attached to the achievement or people walking through produced by an inhabitant's business. Such models show a guarantee to a commonly helpful organization, empowering inhabitant faithfulness.

**Inhabitant Improvement Stipends and Customization**

Furnishing inhabitants with the adaptability to modify their space to suit their business needs is a convincing contribution. Inhabitant Improvement Remittances (TIAs) are reserves designated via landowners to take care of the expenses of alterations or upgrades to the rented space. Offering liberal TIAs can be areas of strength for a for organizations hoping to establish a marked and customized climate.

Working together with inhabitants during the plan and work out process not just guarantees that the space meets their particular prerequisites yet in addition lays out a positive relationship all along. Modified spaces add to occupant fulfillment and can be a conclusive calculate their choice to pick and stay in a specific property.

**Successful Showcasing and Perceivability**

Making mindfulness about the property and its one of a kind contributions is a principal part of occupant fascination. Land owners ought to put resources into compelling promoting techniques to upgrade the perceivability of their business space. This incorporates utilizing advanced advertising channels, keeping a functioning internet based presence, and using web-based entertainment stages to draw in with the interest group.

Cooperative showcasing endeavors with existing inhabitants can likewise be helpful. Joint limited time occasions, cross-showcasing drives, and cooperation in neighborhood local area exercises can hoist the profile of the property and make a positive discernment among expected occupants. The objective is to situate the property as an actual space as well as a dynamic and alluring objective for organizations.

**Innovation Combination and Shrewd Structures**

In a period where innovation assumes a focal part in business tasks, the combination of state of the art innovation inside business properties is turning out to be progressively significant. Land owners can use innovation to upgrade the general occupant experience, work on functional proficiency, and separate their space from others on the lookout.

Brilliant structures furnished with cutting edge robotization, energy the executives frameworks, and incorporated security arrangements add to the general allure of a property. Furthermore, consolidating innovation that upgrades network, like high velocity web and powerful correspondence foundation, is significant for organizations dependent on computerized tasks.

**Supportability Drives**

Supportability has arisen as a critical variable impacting inhabitant choices. Organizations are progressively focusing on naturally capable practices, and land owners can line up with this pattern by carrying out supportability drives inside their turns of events. This could incorporate energy-proficient structure configuration, squander decrease programs, and the utilization of harmless to the ecosystem materials.

Green confirmations, like LEED (Authority in Energy and Natural Plan), can act as a demonstration of a property's obligation to supportability. These certificates appeal to earth cognizant occupants as well as add to the general attractiveness of the property.

**Local area Commitment and Conveniences**

Making a feeling of local area inside a business property is a strong procedure for inhabitant maintenance. Land owners can encourage a cooperative and strong climate by giving common spaces, sorting out systems administration occasions, and working with collaborations among inhabitants. This feeling of local area adds to a good workplace and urges organizations to stay inside the property.

Conveniences assume a critical part in upgrading the general occupant experience. This incorporates shared gathering spaces, wellness focuses, nearby eating choices, and sporting facilities. Mindfully organized conveniences add to the property's engaging quality and can be a game changer for inhabitants thinking about their drawn out obligation to a space.

**Proactive Property The board**

Proactive property the board is fundamental for both inhabitant fascination and maintenance. Responsive and mindful property supervisory groups add to occupant fulfillment by tending to worries expeditiously, keeping up with the property in ideal condition, and encouraging a positive and cooperative relationship with inhabitants.

Normal correspondence is a vital component of proactive property the board. Keeping inhabitants informed about property refreshes, impending occasions, and any important changes shows a promise to straightforwardness and occupant commitment. Furthermore, looking for criticism from occupants and effectively integrating their contribution to property the executives choices supports a cooperative and inhabitant driven approach.

**Occupant Health and Security**

The wellbeing and prosperity of tenants have acquired uplifted significance, especially following worldwide occasions that have underscored the significance of working environment security. Land owners can focus on occupant wellbeing by executing wellbeing and security estimates inside the property. This might include upgraded cleaning conventions, air quality enhancements, and the mix of touchless innovations.

Advancing a free from even a hint of harm climate adds to inhabitant fulfillment and fabricates trust in the property the board's obligation to the prosperity of its tenants. These actions likewise line up with developing assumptions about work environment principles, situating the property as a mindful and inhabitant centered space.

**Normal Market Examination and Flexibility**

The business land scene is dynamic, and economic situations can change quickly. Land owners should direct ordinary market examinations to remain informed about advancing patterns, arising rivalry, and changes in occupant inclinations. This continuous appraisal permits land owners to adjust their procedures proactively and stay receptive to the necessities of the market.

Flexibility is a vital characteristic in effective occupant fascination and maintenance. Whether it includes changing renting structures, consolidating new conveniences, or embracing arising advancements, land owners who stay deft and responsive to change are better situated to explore the difficulties and exploit open doors inside the market.

**4.3 The impact of anchor tenants on the success of a shopping center**

The presence of anchor occupants assumes a crucial part in molding the achievement and practicality of a retail plaza. Anchor occupants, commonly enormous and deep rooted retailers, significantly affect the general presentation, people walking through, and monetary liveliness of a business improvement. In this exhaustive investigation, we will dig into the complex effect of anchor occupants, looking at their impact on the renting elements, the general occupant blend, and the allure of the mall to the two buyers and imminent occupants.

**Anchor Occupants and Renting Elements**

The expression "anchor occupant" alludes to a significant, frequently driving, retailer that fills in as an essential attract for clients to the mall. These inhabitants are decisively situated to draw in critical people strolling through, going about as the foundation around which the remainder of the occupant blend is arranged. The renting elements including anchor occupants are pivotal in laying out the business progress of a retail plaza.

One of the essential advantages of having anchor inhabitants is their capacity to draw a significant number of customers to the middle. Their memorability, far reaching item contributions, and promoting ability add to a consistent inundation of buyers, making a positive expanding influence for more modest, nearby inhabitants. This cooperative energy between anchor inhabitants and more modest retailers encourages a climate where the progress of one supplements the outcome of others.

In renting dealings, anchor occupants frequently appreciate positive terms because of their capacity to drive critical pedestrian activity and upgrade the general attractiveness of the retail plaza.

Landowners might offer cutthroat rental rates, alluring lease terms, and significant inhabitant improvement stipends to get and hold anchor occupants. These renting elements are vital to the monetary outcome of the mall overall.

The dependability given by anchor inhabitants is one more huge part of renting elements. Huge retailers with laid out brands and monetary solidness add to the general validity of the mall. Their presence gives confirmation to different occupants and possible financial backers, flagging a degree of confidence in the business reasonability and long haul supportability of the turn of events.

**Effect on Occupant Blend and Variety**

Anchor occupants assume a pivotal part in molding the inhabitant blend inside a retail plaza. Their size, contributions, and target market impact the determination of different inhabitants to make an assorted and corresponding blend. The objective is to organize an inhabitant blend that requests to an expansive segment, offering a scope of labor and products that take special care of various customer needs and inclinations.

The presence of anchor occupants frequently decides the general subject or focal point of the retail plaza. For instance, a mall moored by a huge retail chain might draw in style retailers, gadgets outlets, and home products stores to supplement the anchor's contributions. This organized blend makes a one-quit shopping objective that urges purchasers to invest more energy investigating different retail choices inside the middle.

Notwithstanding retail, anchor occupants can stretch out their impact to different areas, like eating, amusement, and administrations. A retail plaza secured by a significant supermarket, for example, may draw in cafés, bistros, and other specialist co-ops hoping to gain by the people strolling through produced by the anchor. This expansion upgrades the general buyer experience and adds to the retail outlet's allure as an exhaustive objective.

The effect of anchor inhabitants on occupant blend goes past individual renting arrangements. The presence of a trustworthy anchor can go about as an impetus for drawing in top notch occupants trying to be important for a flourishing and deep rooted business center point. This positive cycle further reinforces the general occupant blend and adds to the seriousness of the mall in the retail market.

**Driving Pedestrian activity and Customer Commitment**

One of the essential elements of anchor inhabitants is to drive pedestrian activity to the retail outlet. Their enormous scope publicizing, limited time exercises, and laid out client base add to a reliable progression of guests. This pedestrian activity isn't just helpful for the anchor inhabitant yet in addition sets out open doors for more modest retailers inside the middle.

Buyers are attracted to retail plazas with anchor occupants because of the accommodation and assortment they offer. The anchor fills in as a point of convergence, drawing in customers who may then investigate contiguous stores and find new retailers. This expanded people walking through benefits all inhabitants, as it upgrades perceivability, builds the potential for motivation buys, and encourages a dynamic and clamoring climate inside the retail plaza.

Anchor occupants frequently sort out special occasions, deals, and showcasing efforts that add to expanded customer commitment. These drives make energy and draw in customers, creating a positive buzz that transmits all through the retail plaza. More modest occupants can use these occasions to exhibit their items or administrations, profiting from the aggregate advertising endeavors drove by the anchor.

**Financial Effect on the Mall**

The monetary effect of anchor occupants reaches out past their singular commitments to the retail plaza's income. The progress of anchor occupants significantly affects the by and large financial strength of the turn of events, the encompassing local area, and the landowner's speculation.

Enormous anchor inhabitants are in many cases significant supporters of the retail plaza's income through their significant rent arrangements, rate based lease structures, and extra expenses for publicizing or shared special exercises. The monetary solidness of anchor inhabitants turns out a dependable revenue stream for landowners, adding to the property's general valuation and engaging quality to financial backers.

The monetary effect isn't restricted to the retail plaza alone; it stretches out to the encompassing local area. The presence of a lively and effective mall makes occupations, animates nearby monetary movement, and can add to expanded property estimations nearby. The financial liveliness produced by anchor occupants has a positive overflow impact that resounds all through the local area.

Also, the outcome of anchor occupants improves the landowner's capacity to get funding and speculation for the retail plaza. Moneylenders and financial backers are many times more leaned to help a property with trustworthy and monetarily stable anchor inhabitants, as their presence mitigates renting dangers and upgrades the generally speaking apparent worth of the venture.

**Difficulties and Contemplations in Anchor Occupant Connections**

While anchor occupants carry significant advantages to malls, their presence additionally presents difficulties and contemplations for land owners and property managers. One test is the likely reliance on a solitary anchor occupant. Depending vigorously on one enormous retailer can make weakness, particularly in the event that that anchor faces monetary hardships, shuts its entryways, or encounters a decrease in fame.

To relieve this gamble, judicious land owners broaden their occupant blend and keep away from overreliance on a solitary anchor. An essential methodology includes getting numerous anchor occupants from various areas, each taking special care of an unmistakable market portion. This expansion supports against the effect of potential difficulties looked by any single anchor inhabitant.

One more thought is the exchange of rent terms with anchor occupants. While property managers might offer good terms to draw in and hold these key occupants, fundamental for figure out some kind of harmony lines up with the monetary objectives of the general mall. Rent arrangements ought to think about elements like rental rates, rent term, co-tenure provisions, and occupant improvement recompenses.

Co-tenure provisos are arrangements in rent arrangements that permit more modest occupants to demand lease decreases or rent end assuming specific circumstances connected with the anchor occupant are not met. These provisions are intended to safeguard more modest occupants if the anchor inhabitant empties or encounters a huge decrease in business.

Also, landowners should cautiously oversee associations with anchor inhabitants to guarantee progressing coordinated effort and arrangement with the mall's general vision. Successful correspondence, cooperative promoting endeavors, and responsiveness to the requirements of anchor inhabitants add to a positive and commonly valuable relationship.

**Adjusting to Changing Retail Patterns**

Despite developing retail drifts, malls should adjust to changing buyer ways of behaving and inclinations. The ascent of web based business, for instance, has prompted shifts in how customers shop, underscoring the significance of making an omnichannel retail insight. Malls with anchor inhabitants need to embrace innovation, coordinate on the web and disconnected procedures, and make consistent encounters that take care of present day buyer assumptions.

Adjusting to changing retail patterns may likewise include rethinking the job of anchor occupants. As opposed to filling in as simple drawcards, anchors can become experiential center points that offer one of a kind and connecting with encounters. This could include incorporating amusement, intuitive presentations, or other experiential components that go past conventional retail.

At times, anchor occupants themselves might develop to fulfill changing buyer needs. Enormous retailers might investigate creative ideas, embrace manageability drives, or enhance their item and administration contributions to stay pertinent in a powerful retail scene. Land owners ought to be receptive to these progressions and team up with anchor occupants to guarantee the mall advances in a state of harmony with arising retail drifts.

The outcome of a mall is a multi-layered accomplishment that depends on a mix of key preparation, powerful administration, and a sharp comprehension of customer conduct. As business scenes develop and shopper inclinations shift, the standards for deciding achievement have extended past simple people walking through and marketing projections. In this exhaustive investigation, we will dig into the different aspects that add to the outcome of a mall, enveloping variables, for example, occupant blend, client experience, innovation coordination, manageability drives, and the flexibility of retail spaces.

**Vital Inhabitant Blend and Broadening**

A basic determinant of a retail plaza's prosperity is the essential curation of its inhabitant blend. The variety and collaboration among occupants assume a critical part in drawing in an expansive scope of buyers and making a far reaching shopping experience. A thoroughly examined occupant blend goes past basically occupying accessible spaces; it includes cautious thought of the kinds of organizations that will complete one another and take special care of the shifted needs and inclinations of the objective segment.

Anchor occupants, frequently huge retailers with laid out brands, act as key attractions that attract critical people strolling through. Their presence not just adds to the general allure of the mall yet additionally impacts the determination of more modest inhabitants. These more modest retailers, thus, add to the energy of the middle by offering a different exhibit of labor and products. The cooperative exchange between anchor occupants and more modest organizations cultivates a climate where each supplements the other, making a convincing objective for shoppers.

The progress of a retail plaza is intently attached to its capacity to adjust its occupant blend to changing business sector patterns. The ascent of web based business, for instance, has prompted the mix of on the web and disconnected retail procedures. Retail plazas that integrate online business monsters or work with snap and-gather administrations exhibit a capacity to embrace advancing shopper ways of behaving. This flexibility guarantees that the occupant blend stays important in a steadily changing retail scene.

**Upgraded Client Experience**

In a time where purchasers look for something beyond a conditional shopping experience, the progress of a mall is complicatedly connected to the nature of client experience it gives. Past the labor and products offered, purchasers esteem a drawing in and charming climate that goes past conventional retail spaces. This accentuation on experience is especially obvious in the advancement of way of life focuses and blended use spaces.

An effective mall makes a climate that urges guests to invest energy, mingle, and investigate. The fuse of common regions, green spaces, and guest plans cultivates a feeling of local area and unwinding.

Besides, the mix of diversion choices, like films, sporting facilities, or far-reaching developments, adds layers to the client experience, making the mall an objective as opposed to a simple value-based space.

Innovation assumes a pivotal part in upgrading client experience. The execution of brilliant innovations, like intuitive presentations, expanded reality, and consistent computerized exchanges, adds to a cutting edge and smoothed out experience. Malls that embrace innovation not just take special care of the inclinations of educated customers yet in addition position themselves as imaginative and ground breaking objections.

Personalization is one more part of client experience that adds to the progress of a retail outlet. Utilizing information examination and client experiences permits malls to fit their contributions and advertising endeavors to individual inclinations. This individual touch makes a more significant association with purchasers and improves the probability of rehash visits.

The progress of a retail outlet is likewise attached to its openness and comfort. Adequate stopping, very much planned walkways, and clear signage add to a positive encounter for guests. The coordination of snap and-gather administrations, curbside pickup choices, and proficient planned operations further upgrade accommodation, taking special care of the speedy ways of life of present day shoppers.

**Incorporation of Innovation and Advancement**

In a time set apart by fast mechanical progressions, the outcome of a mall depends on its capacity to coordinate innovation flawlessly into its tasks. Mechanical advancements upgrade the client experience as well as add to functional productivity, information driven direction, and manageability drives.

The execution of computerized signage, intuitive shows, and increased reality inside a retail plaza establishes a connecting with and dynamic climate. These innovations give open doors to retailers to exhibit items, present customized suggestions, and make vivid brand encounters. Such developments add to the general allure of the retail plaza and position it as a well informed objective.

Web based business combination is a critical part of innovative transformation. Effective malls perceive the significance of spanning the on the web and disconnected retail encounters. This could include giving Wi-Fi availability, supporting versatile application encounters, or working with consistent exchanges that permit shoppers to move easily among physical and advanced channels.

Information examination and man-made brainpower (computer based intelligence) assume a urgent part in molding the progress of a retail plaza. Breaking down customer conduct, buying examples, and segment patterns permits land owners to settle on informed conclusions around

inhabitant blend, advertising systems, and in general property the executives. Simulated intelligence driven advances add to prescient demonstrating, empowering proactive acclimations to meet developing buyer needs.

The utilization of innovation reaches out to functional productivity also. Savvy building the board frameworks, energy-productive advancements, and robotized processes add to maintainable and practical tasks. These developments lessen functional costs as well as position the retail outlet as earth cognizant — a component that reverberates with an inexorably eco-cognizant purchaser base.

Inventive advancements like signal innovation and geofencing add to designated advertising endeavors. These instruments empower customized advancements, continuous notices, and area based impetuses, making a really captivating and significant shopping experience for buyers.

**Supportability Drives**

The outcome of a retail outlet is progressively interwoven with its obligation to maintainability drives. Buyers are putting more prominent accentuation on moral and eco-accommodating practices, and malls that embrace supportability add to natural preservation as well as appeal to a developing business sector fragment.

Green structure rehearses, energy-productive frameworks, and the utilization of maintainable materials add to the eco-accommodating profile of a mall. Accomplishing green confirmations, like LEED (Authority in Energy and Natural Plan), conveys a pledge to manageable turn of events and positions the mall as a capable and ground breaking element.

Squander decrease and reusing programs inside the retail outlet further exhibit a pledge to ecological maintainability. Cooperative endeavors with inhabitants to embrace eco-accommodating practices, like lessening single-use plastics or carrying out energy-effective lighting, add to a comprehensive way to deal with maintainability.

Transportation drives likewise assume a part in the progress of a retail outlet's supportability endeavors. Giving bicycle racks, supporting public transportation choices, and incorporating electric vehicle charging stations add to diminished carbon impressions and line up with the inclinations of earth cognizant shoppers.

Instructive and mindfulness programs inside the retail plaza can additionally enhance the effect of maintainability drives. This could include arranging occasions, studios, or missions that educate customers about the ecological advantages regarding supportable practices and urge them to go with earth cognizant decisions.

Supportability drives are morally mindful as well as monetarily worthwhile. Energy-proficient advances and practices add to cost reserve funds over the long haul, adjusting monetary advantages to natural obligation. Besides, as buyers progressively focus on manageability in their buying choices, malls that embrace green practices gain an upper hand on the lookout.

**Versatility to Changing Retail Patterns**

The retail scene is dynamic, with patterns and buyer inclinations advancing ceaselessly. The outcome of a retail outlet depends on its capacity to adjust to these changes, staying nimble and receptive to arising patterns. From the ascent of web based business to shifts in shopper assumptions, effective malls explore the steadily changing retail scene with foreknowledge and flexibility.

The mix of web based business into the mall experience is a striking variation to changing retail drifts. This includes giving snap and-gather administrations, supporting internet based exchanges, and making consistent omnichannel encounters that overcome any barrier among physical and advanced retail. Retail outlets that embrace these patterns position themselves as flexible and in line with the inclinations of present day buyers.

Adaptability in renting structures is a critical part of adjusting to changing retail drifts. Malls that offer a blend of long haul leases, transient leases, and adaptable spaces take care of the different necessities of retailers in a unique market. This flexibility permits the retail outlet to oblige arising organizations, exploratory ideas, and developing buyer inclinations.

Fruitful retail outlets additionally perceive the developing significance of social business. The coordination of web-based entertainment, force to be reckoned with showcasing, and client produced content into promoting techniques makes a more associated and intuitive shopping experience. By utilizing social business patterns, malls can upgrade their internet based presence, cultivate local area commitment, and drive pedestrian activity to actual stores.

**Local area Commitment and Neighborhood Coordination**

The outcome of a retail outlet is complicatedly connected to its job inside the neighborhood local area. Malls that effectively draw in with and coordinate into the local area are bound to lay out a positive standing, cultivate devotion, and add to the general prosperity of the area.

Local area commitment includes drives that go past customary retail exchanges. Cooperative occasions, organizations with neighborhood associations, and sponsorships of local area exercises add to a positive and coordinated presence inside the local area. This commitment makes a feeling of divided possession and pride between neighborhood inhabitants.

Supporting neighborhood organizations and craftsmans is a critical part of local area joining. Including privately obtained items, facilitating ranchers' business sectors, or giving spaces to neighborhood business visionaries adds to the monetary essentialness of the local area and

adds a particular flavor to the retail outlet. Moreover, supporting nearby organizations cultivates a feeling of credibility and local area character.

Effective retail outlets likewise add to the social advancement of the local area. This could include facilitating widespread developments, workmanship establishments, or exhibitions that feature the variety and imagination of the neighborhood. By becoming social center points, retail plazas improve their allure as objections that offer something beyond business exchanges.

Inclusivity is an indispensable part of local area commitment. Fruitful retail plazas establish conditions that invite different socioeconomics and take special care of an extensive variety of shopper needs. This inclusivity encourages a feeling of having a place and guarantees that the retail plaza stays pertinent and open to the whole local area.

**Proactive Property The board**

The outcome of a retail outlet is dependent upon powerful and proactive property the executives. A very much oversaw property adds to occupant fulfillment, functional effectiveness, and the general engaging quality of the retail plaza to the two inhabitants and purchasers.

Responsive property the executives is fundamental for tending to occupant concerns instantly. Proactive correspondence, standard property support, and proficient issue goal add to a positive connection between land owners and occupants. This positive dynamic, thusly, upgrades inhabitant maintenance and fulfillment.

Inhabitant blend enhancement is a continuous obligation of property the board. Standard appraisals of market patterns, customer inclinations, and the exhibition of individual inhabitants illuminate choices about rent reestablishments, occupant situations, and likely acclimations to the general inhabitant blend. This versatility guarantees that the mall stays significant in a unique market.

Compelling advertising and limited time endeavors are necessary to fruitful property the executives. Facilitated advertising efforts, joint special occasions with inhabitants, and dynamic commitment with the nearby local area add to the general perceivability and attractiveness of the mall. These endeavors draw in buyers as well as make a positive discernment that reverberates with possible occupants.

Notwithstanding everyday tasks, fruitful property the board includes vital anticipating the drawn out supportability of the mall. This could incorporate capital upgrades, redesigns, or the execution of new advances to guarantee that the property stays cutthroat and lined up with developing purchaser assumptions.

# Chapter 5

## Technology Integration in Shopping Centers

The retail scene has gone through a significant change as of late, determined by the persevering progression of innovation. Malls, once inseparable from physical stores and conventional retail encounters, are currently embracing a wide cluster of mechanical developments to remain important and upgrade the general shopping experience. From expanded reality (AR) and augmented reality (VR) to man-made brainpower (computer based intelligence) and the Web of Things (IoT), innovation coordination in malls is reshaping the manner in which purchasers collaborate with actual retail spaces.

One of the critical drivers behind the reception of innovation in malls is the craving to make a consistent and customized shopping venture for buyers. In a period where web based shopping has become progressively famous, malls are utilizing innovation to overcome any issues between the computerized and actual domains. This incorporation not just meets the advancing assumptions for educated buyers yet in addition gives retailers important bits of knowledge into purchaser conduct and inclinations.

Expanded reality has arisen as an incredible asset in changing the customary shopping experience. Retailers are utilizing AR to overlay advanced data onto the actual world, permitting buyers to envision items continuously. For instance, clients can utilize AR applications on their cell phones to perceive how furniture would thoroughly search in their homes prior to making a buy. This improves the shopping experience as well as decreases the probability of profits, as purchasers have a more exact view of the item they are purchasing.

Augmented reality is another innovation causing disturbances in retail outlets. VR establishes vivid conditions that empower customers to investigate items and spaces practically. Some retail plazas are integrating VR into their plan cycle, permitting clients to take virtual voyages through the shopping center or individual stores. This gives a drawing in encounter as well as assists customers with arranging their shopping trips all the more productively.

Man-made brainpower is assuming an essential part in customizing the shopping experience. Computer based intelligence calculations examine tremendous measures of information, including past buy history and online way of behaving, to propose customized proposals to purchasers. Retail plazas are executing man-made intelligence driven chatbots and menial helpers to assist clients with finding items, answer inquiries, and give a more customized and productive shopping experience. These man-made intelligence devices are improving consumer loyalty as well as opening up human staff to zero in on additional perplexing errands.

The Web of Things has additionally tracked down its direction into malls, interfacing actual gadgets and gathering information to improve tasks. Brilliant racks furnished with RFID labels, for example, can screen stock levels continuously, alarming staff while restocking is required. IoT sensors can follow people strolling through inside the shopping center, giving important experiences into purchaser conduct and assisting retailers with arriving at informed conclusions about store formats and item arrangements.

As well as further developing the client experience, innovation combination in retail plazas is smoothing out functional cycles. Portable installment arrangements, for instance, permit clients to make buys with their cell phones, lessening the requirement for actual money or cards. This upgrades accommodation for customers as well as velocities up exchange times, prompting more limited lines and worked on functional proficiency for retailers.

Besides, information examination is assuming a urgent part in molding key choices for malls. By examining information gathered from different touchpoints, including portable applications, virtual entertainment, and in-store sensors, retail plazas can acquire a more profound comprehension of shopper conduct. This information driven approach empowers retailers to streamline stock administration, tailor showcasing methodologies, and make more designated limited time crusades.

The coordination of innovation in malls isn't without its difficulties. Security and security concerns are at the front, as the assortment of immense measures of purchaser information brings up issues about how that data is put away, utilized, and safeguarded. Retail outlets should carry out strong network protection measures to shield delicate client data and fabricate entrust with shoppers who are progressively aware of information security issues.

Moreover, the expense of carrying out and keeping up with trend setting innovations can be a boundary for some retail plazas, especially more modest or freely claimed foundations. In any case, the expected advantages, including expanded people strolling through, higher consumer loyalty, and worked on functional effectiveness, frequently offset the underlying speculation costs.

The job of portable applications in molding the advanced shopping experience couldn't possibly be more significant. Retailers and malls are creating portable applications that offer a scope of elements to upgrade the general client venture. These applications frequently incorporate functionalities, for example, computerized unwaveringness programs, customized offers, and in-application route to assist clients with finding stores and items inside the retail outlet.

Computerized steadfastness programs, coordinated into versatile applications, are an integral asset for encouraging client devotion. These projects commonly offer prizes, limits, or selective admittance to occasions in view of a client's buy history and commitment with the application. By boosting rehash visits and buys, retail plazas can construct enduring associations with their clients.

In-application route highlights influence advancements like geolocation to direct clients through the retail outlet. Clients can include their ideal item classes or explicit stores, and the application gives bit by bit bearings, assisting them with exploring the complicated format of huge retail outlets. This further develops the general client experience as well as supports investigation of various regions inside the shopping center.

Besides, versatile applications empower retail outlets to send message pop-ups to clients in view of their area inside the shopping center. Retailers can utilize this component to convey continuous advancements, limits, or data about continuous occasions straightforwardly to clients' cell phones. This designated approach improves the viability of advertising endeavors and empowers unconstrained buys.

Another pattern picking up speed in malls is the utilization of reference point innovation. Guides are little, Bluetooth-empowered gadgets that can send signs to neighboring cell phones. When coordinated into a mall's framework, reference points can convey area based content and customized offers to clients who have selected in to get such warnings. This innovation makes a hyper-customized shopping experience, with retailers conveying pertinent messages to buyers in light of their continuous area inside the shopping center.

Online entertainment mix is likewise assuming a huge part in the tech-driven change of malls. Numerous retailers and malls have embraced online entertainment stages as strong advertising instruments to interface with clients and advance their image. Web-based entertainment channels are utilized for publicizing as well as stages for drawing in with clients progressively.

Retail plazas influence virtual entertainment to report advancements, share in the background content, and associate with their crowd. Client produced content, for example, photographs and surveys shared by clients, is in many cases highlighted on true mall profiles, making a feeling of local area and validness. This online entertainment presence assists work with marking faithfulness and urges clients to share their own encounters, successfully becoming supporters for the mall.

Live streaming is one more creative way to deal with online entertainment combination in malls. Retailers can utilize live streaming stages to feature new items, direct virtual voyages through stores, or even host intuitive occasions. This constant commitment permits retail outlets to interface with their crowd on a more profound level, making a more powerful and vivid internet based insight.

Besides, social trade is turning out to be progressively predominant in malls' advanced techniques. Stages like Instagram and Facebook have incorporated shopping functionalities, permitting clients to find and buy items straightforwardly inside the online entertainment application. Malls can use these elements to contact a more extensive crowd and drive on the web and disconnected deals at the same time.

The idea of a shrewd retail outlet is building up some forward momentum as innovation keeps on progressing. A savvy mall coordinates different innovations to establish an associated and proficient retail climate. Savvy framework, including IoT gadgets and sensors, shapes the foundation of these turns of events, empowering ongoing information assortment and examination for further developed independent direction.

Savvy stopping is one part of a shrewd retail outlet that improves the general client experience. IoT sensors in parking areas can give continuous data about accessible parking spots, assisting clients with finding stopping rapidly and decreasing blockage. Some savvy retail outlets considerably offer held parking spots for application clients, further boosting the utilization of portable applications.

Shrewd lighting is another element that adds to the proficiency and supportability of malls. Robotized lighting frameworks can change splendor in view of normal light circumstances and pedestrian activity, streamlining energy utilization. Also, these frameworks can make customized lighting situations to upgrade the climate in various region of the retail plaza.

The mix of facial acknowledgment innovation is likewise causing disturbances in savvy retail outlets. Facial acknowledgment can be utilized for different purposes, including access control, customized client encounters, and security. Some retail plazas are investigating the execution of facial acknowledgment for installment confirmation, permitting clients to make buys by just checking their countenances.

Besides, the idea of an associated store is reshaping individual retail spaces inside malls. Associated stores influence innovation to make a consistent and incorporated shopping experience for clients. RFID innovation, for example, can be utilized to follow items inside the store, giving ongoing stock data to the two clients and staff. This guarantees that clients can undoubtedly find the items they are searching for and that the store can effectively deal with its stock levels.

Brilliant mirrors are one more creative component in associated stores. These mirrors utilize increased reality innovation to permit clients to for all intents and purposes take a stab at dress things without truly changing into them. This improves the shopping experience as well as diminishes the requirement for fitting rooms, smoothing out the general cycle and limiting sit tight times for clients.

As well as improving the client experience, associated stores likewise furnish retailers with important information on client conduct. By following how clients collaborate with items and store designs, retailers can pursue information driven choices to enhance the shopping climate and further develop deals. This information can likewise be utilized to customize advertising endeavors and advancements.

The mix of innovation in malls reaches out past individual stores and client confronting applications. Back-end frameworks, including stock administration, inventory network coordinated factors, and representative preparation, are additionally profiting from mechanical headways. Distributed computing, for instance, empowers malls to incorporate information stockpiling and handling, working with constant joint effort and data sharing across the whole retail biological system.

Production network streamlining is a basic part of innovation joining in retail outlets. RFID innovation, specifically, is being utilized to further develop stock precision and lessen unavailable circumstances. By labeling items with RFID labels, retailers can follow the development of things all through the inventory network, from distribution centers to stores. This perceivability empowers more effective stock administration and limits the gamble of stockouts.

Besides, prescient examination is assuming a key part in production network streamlining. By investigating authentic information and outside factors, retailers can figure request all the more precisely, considering better stock preparation and recharging.

This proactive methodology diminishes overabundance stock, limit squander, and guarantee that well known items are reliably accessible to clients.

Worker preparing and advancement are additionally being changed by innovation in retail outlets. Computer generated reality is being utilized to recreate sensible situations for preparing, permitting representatives to rehearse errands in a controlled and vivid climate. This upgrades the viability of preparing programs as well as decreases the requirement for actual preparation spaces and materials.

The utilization of mechanical technology is one more pattern in the enhancement of back-end processes in retail outlets. Independent robots can be sent for undertakings, for example, stock examining, floor cleaning, and even client support. These robots increment proficiency as well as let loose human representatives to zero in on additional complex and worth added errands.

As malls keep on embracing innovation, manageability is turning into an undeniably significant thought. Green advances and eco-accommodating practices are being incorporated into the plan and activity of retail plazas to limit natural effect. For instance, shrewd energy the board frameworks can improve the utilization of lighting, warming, and cooling, decreasing in general energy utilization.

Besides, some retail outlets are integrating sustainable power sources, like sunlight based chargers, to produce power. This lessens the natural impression as well as brings down energy costs over the long haul. Feasible materials and development rehearses are additionally acquiring notoriety, with retail plazas intending to limit squander and make more eco-accommodating spaces.

All in all, innovation reconciliation in malls is a complex peculiarity that is reshaping the retail scene. From upgrading the client experience with expanded reality and portable applications to enhancing back-end processes with IoT and man-made brainpower, innovation is assuming a significant part in the development of retail outlets. As the speed of mechanical development keeps on speeding up, malls that hug and adjust to these progressions are probably going to flourish in the dynamic and cutthroat universe of retail. The critical lies in tracking down the right harmony between mechanical progressions, client assumptions, and manageable practices to establish a shopping climate that isn't just mechanically progressed yet in addition client driven and naturally cognizant.

## 5.1 The role of technology in enhancing the shopping experience

In the steadily developing scene of retail, innovation has turned into a main impetus reshaping the manner in which shoppers communicate with brands and settle on buying choices. The mix of innovation in shopping conditions has changed the conventional shopping experience as well as turned into a basic component for retailers hoping to remain serious in a quickly evolving market.

From online stages to physical stores, the job of innovation in improving the shopping experience is diverse and keeps on developing with progressions in computerized advancement.

One of the central ways innovation improves the shopping experience is through the ascent of internet business stages. Web based shopping has turned into an omnipresent piece of present day customer conduct, offering comfort, assortment, and openness. Web based business stages give buyers the capacity to peruse and buy items from the solace of their homes, taking out the requirement for actual travel to retail stores. This comfort factor has reshaped the retail scene, provoking conventional physical stores to adjust and coordinate innovation to stay pertinent.

Cell phones, especially cell phones and tablets, assume a focal part in the consistent coordination of innovation into the shopping experience. Versatile applications created by retailers act as amazing assets to interface with purchasers, giving highlights like customized suggestions, selective arrangements, and simple route through virtual inventories. These applications work with the shopping system as well as empower retailers to accumulate important information on purchaser inclinations and conduct, adding to more designated advertising techniques.

Increased reality (AR) and computer generated reality (VR) are state of the art innovations that carry an intelligent and vivid aspect to the shopping experience. AR overlays advanced data onto this present reality, improving the actual climate with extra layers of information. Retailers influence AR to empower clients to basically take a stab at dress or frill, envision furniture in their homes, or even perceive how cosmetics items will look on their countenances. This innovation overcomes any issues between the on the web and disconnected shopping encounters, furnishing customers with a more educated and connecting method for pursuing buy choices.

Essentially, VR takes the shopping experience to another level by establishing completely virtual conditions. A few retailers and brands use VR to reenact genuine situations, permitting clients to investigate items or administrations in a virtual space. This innovation is especially important in areas like land, where potential purchasers can take virtual voyages through properties without truly visiting the areas. VR changes the shopping experience from a value-based process into a vivid excursion, cultivating a more profound association between the brand and the buyer.

Man-made brainpower (simulated intelligence) is one more significant innovation driving the improvement of the shopping experience. Computer based intelligence calculations dissect immense measures of information to grasp customer conduct, inclinations, and patterns. Retailers use simulated intelligence to give customized proposals, foresee purchaser needs, and enhance estimating techniques.

Chatbots fueled by man-made intelligence are utilized to help clients progressively, noting questions, offering item data, and working with the buying system. These computer based intelligence driven cooperations add to a more proficient and customized shopping experience.

The Web of Things (IoT) has pervaded the retail space, interfacing actual gadgets and making an organization of shrewd, interconnected frameworks. Brilliant racks outfitted with RFID labels empower retailers to screen stock levels progressively, diminishing occurrences of stockouts and overload. IoT sensors can follow client developments inside stores, giving experiences into people strolling through designs and well known shopping regions. This information driven approach engages retailers to streamline store formats, upgrade item arrangements, and work on the general progression of the shopping experience.

Notwithstanding these innovative headways, the idea of a consistent and contactless installment experience has acquired conspicuousness. Versatile installment arrangements, computerized wallets, and contactless installment techniques have become fundamental parts of the cutting edge shopping venture. These advances offer accommodation as well as address concerns connected with cleanliness and security, especially with regards to worldwide occasions that accentuate the significance of limiting actual contact.

Moreover, the mix of innovation in actual retail spaces has led to the idea of the "brilliant store." Savvy stores influence IoT, sensors, and different advancements to establish a wise and responsive climate. For example, shrewd mirrors furnished with RFID innovation can perceive the dress things clients bring into fitting rooms and recommend correlative items or embellishments. Intuitive presentations and touchscreens give extra item data, styling tips, and client audits, advancing the by and large in-store insight.

Personalization is a vital component in the mechanical development of the shopping experience. Retailers bridle information investigation and simulated intelligence to figure out individual inclinations and ways of behaving, taking into consideration profoundly focused on and customized promoting endeavors. Customized proposals, custom-made advancements, and individualized shopping encounters add to consumer loyalty and devotion. The capacity to expect and satisfy the remarkable requirements of every client enjoys become a cutthroat benefit in the retail scene.

Web-based entertainment stages assume a huge part in the reconciliation of innovation into the shopping experience. Retailers influence online entertainment for brand advancement, client commitment, and direct correspondence with their crowd. Social trade, the combination of web-based entertainment and online business, empowers customers to find, investigate, and buy items straightforwardly through virtual entertainment stages. Shopping highlights incorporated into stages like Instagram and Facebook permit clients to consistently progress from item disclosure to exchange inside the equivalent application, making a smoothed out and vivid shopping experience.

Live streaming has arisen as a dynamic and intelligent way for retailers to interface with their crowd continuously. Retailers utilize live gushing to exhibit item dispatches, direct virtual occasions, and draw in with clients through back and forth discussions. This constant collaboration fabricates a feeling of local area and credibility, cultivating a more grounded association between the brand and its crowd. Live streaming likewise gives an open door to buyers to see items in real life, upgrading their comprehension and trust in going with buying choices.

The idea of experiential retail has gotten some forward momentum as innovation keeps on molding the shopping scene. Experiential retail goes past conventional exchanges, zeroing in on making paramount and vivid encounters for clients. Retailers configuration spaces that connect with the faculties, consolidating components like intuitive showcases, advanced workmanship establishments, and even fragrance or sound encounters. These tangible rich conditions draw in clients as well as make an enduring impression, empowering rehash visits and positive verbal.

The job of innovation in improving the shopping experience stretches out to the production network and planned operations. Effective and straightforward inventory network the board is basic for guaranteeing that items are accessible when and where clients need them. Innovations, for example, blockchain are being investigated to make a decentralized and secure record of the inventory network, giving perceivability into the excursion of items from creation to the store racks. This straightforwardness further develops discernibility as well as fabricates trust among buyers who are progressively intrigued by the beginnings and supportability of the items they buy.

Mechanical computerization is making huge commitments to the effectiveness of inventory network activities. Independent robots can be sent in stockrooms for errands, for example, request picking, pressing, and stock administration. These robots improve speed and exactness, diminishing the time it takes to satisfy orders and limiting blunders all the while. The outcome is a more smoothed out store network that satisfies the needs of the present speedy and dynamic retail climate.

The coordination of innovation in the shopping experience isn't without challenges. Security and protection concerns are fundamental, particularly with the assortment and capacity of huge measures of buyer information. Retailers should focus on vigorous network safety measures to safeguard delicate data and construct entrust with clients. Finding some kind of harmony among personalization and protection is a continuous test, requiring cautious thought and adherence to moral information rehearses.

Also, there is the test of inclusivity and availability. While innovation can possibly improve the shopping experience for some, it's urgent to guarantee that these progressions are open to all purchasers, incorporating those with inabilities or restricted mechanical education.

Retailers need to consider comprehensive plan standards to guarantee that their mechanical developments are usable and valuable for a different scope of clients.

## 5.2 Use of augmented reality, virtual reality, and smart technology

The utilization of increased reality (AR), computer generated reality (VR), and brilliant innovation has significantly changed different enterprises, altering the manner in which we collaborate with our general surroundings. From diversion and training to medical services and retail, these advancements have opened up additional opportunities and improved our encounters. In this investigation, we dive into the applications and effect of expanded reality, augmented reality, and brilliant innovation across various areas.

Increased reality (AR) is an innovation that overlays computerized data or virtual components onto this present reality, improving our insight and connection with the climate. In the domain of training, AR has turned into an important device for vivid growth opportunities. Instructive applications and stages use AR to rejuvenate reading material, permitting understudies to investigate 3D models, intelligent reenactments, and extra satisfied connected with their illustrations. This makes learning more captivating as well as helps in better cognizance and maintenance of data.

Also, AR has tracked down applications in medical services, adding to clinical preparation and patient consideration. Clinical understudies can utilize AR recreations to rehearse medical procedures and methodology in a gamble free virtual climate. Specialists, then again, can use AR during genuine medical procedures for constant direction and perception of basic data, like patient information or the area of inward designs. AR upgrades accuracy and dynamic in clinical settings, eventually working on persistent results.

In the retail area, AR is reshaping the client shopping experience. Retailers use AR applications to permit clients to practically take a stab at dress and frill, picture furniture in their homes prior to buying, or even perceive how cosmetics items will look on their skin. This mixing of the computerized and actual domains makes a more intelligent and customized shopping venture, diminishing the requirement for actual attempt ons and improving consumer loyalty.

Computer generated reality (VR), then again, drenches clients in totally virtual conditions, making a reproduced reality that can be investigated and communicated with. VR has turned into an integral asset for preparing and recreation across different ventures. In flight, pilots use VR reproductions to work on flying under various circumstances, upgrading their abilities and readiness for true situations. Likewise, VR is utilized in military preparation, permitting officers to reenact battle circumstances and practice dynamic in a controlled climate.

Training has likewise embraced computer generated simulation as a groundbreaking learning instrument. VR reenactments can ship understudies to verifiable occasions, distant areas, or even inside the human body, giving a degree of drenching that conventional strategies can't

coordinate. This experiential learning approach cultivates further comprehension and commitment, making complex subjects more available and pleasant for understudies.

In medical care, VR is used for helpful purposes, especially in torment the executives and emotional well-being therapy. VR conditions can divert patients from torment during operations or recovery works out. Moreover, VR treatment is utilized to treat conditions, for example, post-horrendous pressure problem (PTSD) and nervousness by presenting people to controlled and vivid situations that help them defy and deal with their feelings of dread.

Media outlets has been at the very front of taking on computer generated simulation to make vivid and spellbinding encounters. VR gaming, specifically, has acquired fame, offering players a phenomenal degree of cooperation and commitment. Past gaming, VR is being utilized to make virtual shows, gallery visits, and different types of diversion that transport clients to intriguing universes without leaving their homes.

The intermingling of expanded reality and augmented reality, frequently alluded to as blended the truth, is pushing the limits of what is conceivable. Blended reality consolidates the genuine and virtual universes in a consistent way, permitting clients to at the same time cooperate with the two conditions. In businesses like engineering and configuration, blended the truth is utilized to envision and control 3D models progressively, empowering planners and architects to settle on informed conclusions about spaces and designs.

The utilization of brilliant innovation, which incorporates a scope of interconnected gadgets and frameworks, has become vital to our regular routines. Shrewd homes, furnished with associated gadgets and computerization frameworks, offer inhabitants remarkable command over their residing spaces. Shrewd indoor regulators, lighting, surveillance cameras, and voice-enacted associates improve solace, security, and productivity. The Web of Things (IoT) assumes a critical part in empowering these gadgets to convey and cooperate consistently.

In medical services, brilliant innovation is working on persistent consideration and the board. Wearable gadgets, like wellness trackers and smartwatches, screen imperative signs, track action levels, and give constant wellbeing information. This data permits people to adopt a proactive strategy to their prosperity, while medical services suppliers can involve it for more customized and preventive consideration.

Furthermore, brilliant clinical gadgets, similar to insulin siphons and ceaseless glucose screens, enable people with persistent circumstances to actually deal with their well-being more.

Brilliant innovation has reformed transportation through the improvement of independent vehicles and savvy framework. Self-driving vehicles utilize a mix of sensors, cameras, and simulated intelligence calculations to explore streets and simply decide.

Shrewd urban areas influence innovation to upgrade transportation frameworks, lessen gridlock, and work on generally metropolitan effectiveness. Associated vehicles and traffic the board frameworks empower constant information trade, upgrading courses and limiting natural effect.

In the domain of horticulture, savvy innovation is driving accuracy cultivating rehearses. IoT sensors gather information on soil wellbeing, atmospheric conditions, and yield development, permitting ranchers to come to informed conclusions about water system, preparation, and bug control. Drones furnished with imaging innovation give airborne perspectives on fields, assisting ranchers with checking crops and recognize issues almost immediately. This information driven approach upgrades crop yield, diminishes asset squander, and advances economical cultivating rehearses.

The retail business has embraced savvy innovation to smooth out activities and improve the client experience. Brilliant stock administration frameworks use RFID labels and sensors to screen item levels continuously, diminishing occasions of stockouts and overload. Guides and area based innovation give customized advancements and limits to clients in light of their ongoing area inside a store. Furthermore, brilliant checkout frameworks, for example, clerk less stores, take out the requirement for conventional clerks, accelerating the buying system.

The arrangement of brilliant innovation in assembling, known as Industry 4.0, is changing creation cycles and production network the board. Associated machines and sensors accumulate information on gear execution, empowering prescient support and limiting free time. Shrewd industrial facilities influence computerization, advanced mechanics, and information investigation to streamline creation proficiency, diminish squander, and answer rapidly to changing business sector requests.

The idea of brilliant urban areas imagines metropolitan conditions that influence innovation to improve maintainability, proficiency, and the personal satisfaction for inhabitants. Brilliant city drives incorporate a scope of uses, including savvy energy frameworks, squander the board frameworks, and public transportation. IoT sensors and information examination empower city authorities to screen and oversee assets continuously, prompting more educated direction and worked on metropolitan preparation.

In any case, the broad reception of expanded reality, augmented reality, and shrewd innovation isn't without challenges. Protection and security concerns emerge as these advancements include the assortment and examination of tremendous measures of individual information. Finding some kind of harmony among advancement and protecting people's security is pivotal to building trust in the utilization of these innovations.

Interoperability is another test, especially with regards to savvy innovation. The expansion of gadgets and frameworks from various makers can bring about similarity issues and frustrate consistent mix. Normalization endeavors and open-source stages expect to address these difficulties, encouraging a more interconnected and interoperable biological system.

Besides, the computerized partition stays a worry, as admittance to these innovations isn't uniform across populaces. Financial variables, geographic area, and framework differences can make disparities in admittance to expanded reality, computer generated reality, and shrewd innovation. Endeavors to connect this gap and guarantee inclusivity in the reception of these advances are fundamental for understanding their maximum capacity.

Taking everything into account, the utilization of increased reality, computer generated reality, and shrewd innovation has reclassified the manner in which we collaborate with the world and can possibly keep forming different enterprises. From upgrading instruction and medical care to altering amusement, transportation, and metropolitan living, these advances offer creative answers for complex difficulties. As we explore the potential open doors and difficulties introduced by these headways, a smart and moral methodology is fundamental for saddle the full advantages while addressing concerns connected with protection, security, and inclusivity.

### 5.3 E-commerce integration and click-and-collect services

In the powerful scene of retail, the coordination of web based business and the ascent of snap and-gather administrations have reshaped the manner in which customers shop and organizations work. This advancement mirrors the developing impact of computerized innovations on the retail area, bringing accommodation, adaptability, and effectiveness to the very front. In this investigation, we dive into the complexities of web based business mix and the rise of snap and-gather administrations, analyzing their effect on the two buyers and retailers.

**Web based business Coordination:**

Web based business, short for electronic trade, alludes to the trading of labor and products over the web. The coordination of web based business into conventional retail models has been a groundbreaking power, separating geological hindrances and offering purchasers uncommon admittance to a worldwide commercial center. This joining includes the consistent intermingling of on the web and disconnected channels, making a firm shopping experience for clients.

One of the critical parts of web based business coordination is the improvement of online stages and sites that act as advanced customer facing facades for organizations. These stages give a virtual space where retailers can feature their items, offer itemized data, and work with exchanges. Shoppers, thus, can peruse a huge swath of items, look at costs, read surveys, and make buys — all from the solace of their homes or in a hurry through cell phones.

The incorporation of web based business reaches out past the computerized customer facing facade to incorporate different elements and functionalities pointed toward upgrading the internet shopping experience. Customized proposals, in light of calculations breaking down past buys and perusing conduct, assist purchasers with finding items custom-made to their inclinations. High level pursuit capacities and channels empower clients to effectively explore broad item indexes, reducing choices to rapidly track down the ideal things.

Installment doors assume a urgent part in working with secure and consistent exchanges in the domain of online business. Incorporating different installment choices, including charge cards, computerized wallets, and other web-based installment strategies, guarantees that clients can pick the installment technique generally advantageous for them. Also, the execution of secure encryption innovations shields touchy monetary data, building trust and certainty among online customers.

The coordinated factors and satisfaction part of web based business reconciliation is a basic part that straightforwardly impacts the client experience. Proficient request handling, precise stock administration, and opportune conveyance are fundamental for meeting client assumptions. Numerous online business stages influence progressed production network innovations, for example, stockroom computerization and request global positioning frameworks, to improve these cycles and give continuous perceivability into the situation with orders.

Moreover, the mix of web based business frequently reaches out to client relationship the executives (CRM) frameworks. These frameworks empower organizations to follow client associations, oversee correspondence, and assemble important information for the purpose of advertising. By investigating client conduct and inclinations, organizations can tailor showcasing efforts, advancements, and dedication programs, cultivating a more customized and drawing in relationship with their crowd.

The idea of omnichannel retailing is intently attached to web based business reconciliation, underlining a consistent and reliable shopping experience across different channels. Buyers today anticipate that the adaptability should progress easily among on the web and disconnected touchpoints. Retailers that effectively coordinate web based business into their general technique can offer a brought together encounter, permitting clients to peruse on the web, make buys coming up, as well as the other way around, with a strong and interconnected venture.

Be that as it may, web based business combination isn't without challenges. Security and protection concerns are foremost, given the touchy idea of the data traded during on the web exchanges. Retailers should execute powerful network safety measures to safeguard client information, fabricate trust, and consent to information security guidelines.

Furthermore, the requirement for nonstop mechanical updates and transformations to developing shopper assumptions represents a continuous test for organizations embracing internet business combination.

**Snap and-Gather Administrations:**

The ascent of snap and-gather administrations addresses a significant change in the manner buyers decide to get and gather their web-based buys. Snap and-gather, otherwise called "purchase on the web, get coming up" (BOPIS), permits clients to cause buys on the web and afterward to recover their things at an actual store area or assigned pickup point. This half and half methodology joins the comfort of web based shopping with the quickness of in-store pickup, taking special care of the inclinations of present day purchasers.

One of the essential advantages of snap and-gather administrations is the adaptability it offers to shoppers. Customers can peruse and make buys whenever the timing is ideal through web-based stages, and on second thought of sitting tight for home conveyance, they can select to gather their things when it suits them. This adaptability is especially engaging for people with occupied plans, giving an option in contrast to conventional transportation that may not line up with their accessibility.

The snap and-gather model is profitable for retailers also. It tends to difficulties related with last-mile conveyance, where the expense and operations of arriving at individual families can be mind boggling. By empowering clients to get their orders coming up, retailers can improve their production network and diminish the stress on conveyance organizations. This productivity can bring about cost reserve funds for both the retailer and the buyer.

Notwithstanding cost reserve funds, snap and-gather administrations add to expanded people strolling through in actual stores. At the point when clients come to gather their orders, they might be leaned to make extra in-store buys, prompting upselling amazing open doors. This mixing of on the web and disconnected exchanges cultivates a cooperative connection between internet business and physical retail, utilizing the qualities of each channel to improve generally deals and client commitment.

The snap and-gather model likewise resolves the issue of missed conveyances, a typical dissatisfaction for online customers. By giving a pickup choice, retailers moderate the bother of bombed conveyance endeavors and the likely requirement for clients to improve their timetables to get bundles. This comfort lines up with the assumptions for the present buyers, who esteem adaptability and command over their shopping experience.

Besides, snap and-gather administrations can add to a more manageable and eco-accommodating way to deal with retail. By solidifying orders for in-store pickup, retailers can streamline conveyance courses and decrease the carbon impression related with individual home conveyances. This lines up with the developing mindfulness and worry for natural manageability, reverberating with shoppers who focus on eco-cognizant practices.

The progress of snap and-gather administrations depends vigorously on the consistent coordination of on the web and disconnected frameworks. Stock administration should be exact and exceptional to keep away from issues, for example, stockouts or overpromising on item accessibility. Continuous correspondence between the internet based stage and actual stores is fundamental to guarantee that clients get opportune notices about the situation with their orders and the accessibility of things for pickup.

Nonetheless, challenges exist in the execution of snap and-gather administrations. Functional intricacies, including the requirement for assigned pickup regions, prepared staff, and productive request handling, require cautious preparation and execution. The client experience during the pickup interaction is urgent, and any deferrals or errors can decrease the benefits of snap and-gather and lead to disappointment.

Besides, the progress of snap and-gather administrations is dependent upon a consistent and easy to understand online stage. The site or application should give clear data about item accessibility, pickup areas, and the means engaged with the cycle. Any grating or disarray in the web-based experience can prevent clients from picking the snap and-gather choice.

**The Future Scene:**

Looking forward, the coordination of online business and the advancement of snap and-gather administrations are supposed to keep molding the retail scene. Propels in innovation, including the utilization of man-made consciousness (computer based intelligence) and AI, will probably assume a huge part in further streamlining online business stages. Customized proposals, further developed search calculations, and improved client collaborations are regions where man-made intelligence can add to a more consistent and custom-made internet shopping experience.

The development of portable trade, worked with by cell phones and other cell phones, will likewise impact the fate of web based business joining. Versatile appli cations offer a helpful way for buyers to peruse, shop, and draw in with brands in a hurry. Retailers should focus on versatile improvement and make responsive, easy to use connection points to take care of the rising number of clients getting to web based business stages through cell phones.

In the domain of snap and-gather administrations, advancements in planned operations and satisfaction innovations will probably address existing difficulties and upgrade the productivity of in-store pickups. Robotization, mechanical technology, and high level global positioning frameworks can add to quicker arrange handling and further developed correspondence between online stages and actual stores. The incorporation of these advancements might make ready for new models of snap and-gather, for example, computerized storage frameworks and smoothed out pickup processes.

The job of information investigation will turn out to be more articulated in both online business reconciliation and snap and-gather administrations. Retailers can use information to acquire experiences into client conduct, inclinations, and patterns. This data can illuminate stock administration, showcasing techniques, and the improvement of customized advancements, making a more designated and client driven way to deal with retail.

As supportability turns into an undeniably basic thought, retailers might investigate eco-accommodating practices in online business and snap and-gather activities. From enhancing conveyance courses to executing green bundling arrangements, ecologically cognizant drives can line up with shopper esteems and add to a positive brand picture.

The continuous combination of on the web and disconnected retail encounters will probably prompt new models that flawlessly mix the upsides of the two channels. Ideas like experiential retail, where actual stores offer vivid and drawing in encounters, may supplement the comfort of online business. Retailers might explore different avenues regarding imaginative advances, like expanded reality, to make virtual take a stab at encounters or upgrade the in-store venture for clients.

# Chapter 6

### Sustainability in Shopping Centers

Maintainability in malls has turned into an essential concentration in the cutting edge period, as organizations and shoppers the same perceive the requirement for ecologically cognizant practices. The retail business, with its rambling shopping centers and edifices, altogether affects the climate, from asset utilization to squander age. Subsequently, there is a developing accentuation on incorporating supportable practices into the plan, development, and activity of retail plazas.

One of the vital parts of maintainable retail outlets is the accentuation on eco-accommodating engineering and plan. Conventional malls frequently focus on style and usefulness disregarding the ecological effect. Manageable malls, then again, focus on green structure rehearses, energy productivity, and the utilization of eco-accommodating materials.

Green structure rehearses include planning and developing designs that limit adverse consequences on the climate. This incorporates utilizing inexhaustible and reused materials, consolidating energy-proficient advances, and planning spaces that enhance normal light and ventilation. Maintainable malls frequently include green rooftops, water gathering frameworks, and energy-proficient lighting to lessen their carbon impression.

Notwithstanding eco-accommodating design, feasible retail plazas center around the dependable utilization of assets. This incorporates limiting water utilization, decreasing energy use, and overseeing waste successfully. Numerous cutting edge malls put resources into trend setting innovations to screen and advance asset utilization, from savvy lighting frameworks to water reusing drives.

Energy effectiveness is a basic part of supportable malls. These buildings consume immense measures of energy for lighting, warming, and cooling. To address this, maintainable retail plazas incorporate energy-proficient advances like Drove lighting, sunlight powered chargers, and savvy air conditioning frameworks. These actions lessen the natural effect as well as add to cost investment funds over the long haul.

Water preservation is one more huge thought in feasible mall plan. Conventional malls frequently have high water utilization because of arranging needs, bathrooms, and different offices. Feasible options incorporate water-effective arranging, low-stream installations, and the utilization of reused water for non-consumable purposes. By taking on these works on, retail plazas can add to nearby water protection endeavors.

Squander the executives is a significant part of manageability in malls. Customary shopping centers create significant measures of waste, including bundling materials, food squander, and different disposables. Reasonable malls execute complete reusing programs, urge retailers to limit bundling, and integrate squander to-energy advances to decrease the by and large natural effect.

Additionally, maintainable retail outlets effectively advance and backing earth dependable practices among their inhabitants. They may boost retailers to embrace eco-accommodating bundling, carry out reusing drives, and participate in supportable strategic approaches. Some retail plazas even give instructive projects to bring issues to light among inhabitants and purchasers about the significance of maintainability.

Transportation is a vital thought in the manageability of malls. Conventional shopping centers frequently add to gridlock and air contamination because of their area and plan. Supportable retail outlets focus on availability through open transportation, bicycle paths, and person on foot agreeable pathways. Moreover, a retail outlets offer electric vehicle charging stations to empower the utilization of eco-accommodating transportation choices.

The joining of innovation assumes a critical part in improving maintainability in retail outlets. Brilliant structure frameworks, IoT (Web of Things) sensors, and information examination add to productive asset the board. For instance, sensors can screen inhabitance levels to upgrade lighting and air conditioning frameworks, while information investigation can distinguish regions for additional energy and water preservation.

Besides, feasible retail outlets embrace the idea of blended use advancement. As opposed to being independent designs centered exclusively around retail, these edifices incorporate private, office, and sporting spaces. This approach diminishes the requirement for broad driving, advances a feeling of local area, and expands the usage of room in an ecologically capable way.

Local area commitment is an essential part of practical retail outlets. These edifices effectively include the neighborhood local area in their drives and dynamic cycles. This can incorporate effort programs, associations with neighborhood associations, and local area occasions zeroed in on supportability and ecological training. By encouraging a feeling of shared liability, reasonable retail outlets become essential pieces of the networks they serve.

Certificates and norms likewise assume a part in advancing maintainability in retail outlets. Different associations offer certificates for harmless to the ecosystem structures, like LEED (Administration in Energy and Natural Plan). Accomplishing such confirmations exhibits a promise to reasonable practices and gives a benchmark to persistent improvement.

The financial part of supportability isn't disregarded in that frame of mind of retail outlets. While there might be an underlying interest in eco-accommodating advances and plan, the drawn out benefits frequently offset the expenses. Energy-productive frameworks lead to bring down functional costs, and feasible practices can draw in earth cognizant purchasers and occupants, adding to the generally speaking financial feasibility of the mall.

Customer training is a basic part of advancing manageability in retail plazas. Numerous customers are progressively aware of their natural effect and really like to help organizations that line up with their qualities. Supportable retail outlets influence this mindfulness by giving data about their green drives, advancing eco-accommodating items, and empowering dependable customer conduct.

Retailers inside economical malls likewise assume a critical part in propelling manageability. These organizations are urged to take on harmless to the ecosystem rehearses, for example, obtaining items capably, limiting bundling, and executing reusing programs. Malls can team up with retailers to lay out manageability rules and perceive and compensate organizations that effectively add to the generally speaking ecological objectives.

All in all, maintainability in malls envelops a comprehensive methodology that coordinates eco-accommodating design, mindful asset the board, local area commitment, and innovation driven proficiency. As the world keeps on wrestling with natural difficulties, the retail business has a novel chance to show others how its done and add to a more reasonable future. Manageable retail outlets limit their natural impression as well as make spaces that focus on the prosperity of networks, shoppers, and the planet overall. As the interest for manageable practices keeps on developing, the job of retail outlets in molding a greener, more dependable future turns out to be progressively critical.

### 6.1 Green building practices in shopping center construction

Green structure rehearses in retail plaza development have arisen as an essential system to address ecological worries and advance reasonable turn of events. The development business, with its significant effect on asset utilization, energy use, and waste age, assumes a critical part in molding the maintainability of constructed conditions. In this unique circumstance, malls, as mind boggling structures that house various retail spaces, can possibly essentially impact natural results through the reception of green structure rehearses.

An essential part of green structure rehearses in mall development includes the choice of eco-accommodating materials. Conventional development frequently depends on asset escalated materials with huge ecological impressions. Green structure, then again, stresses the utilization of feasible materials like reused steel, recovered wood, and low-influence concrete. These materials diminish the interest for virgin assets as well as add to limiting the natural effect of development.

The plan period of retail plaza development is a basic chance to incorporate maintainability standards. Green structure rehearses focus on plans that upgrade regular light and ventilation, diminishing the requirement for fake lighting and mechanical ventilation. This diminishes energy utilization as well as improves the indoor climate, making more agreeable and welcoming spaces for customers and inhabitants.

Besides, economical retail outlet development integrates energy-effective advances to limit the natural effect of energy utilization. This incorporates the utilization of energy-effective lighting frameworks, high level central air (warming, ventilation, and cooling) frameworks, and shrewd structure controls. These advances decrease energy utilization during activity as well as add to long haul cost investment funds for retail outlet proprietors and inhabitants.

The development business is a critical supporter of ozone harming substance emanations, principally through energy-concentrated cycles like concrete creation. Green structure rehearses in mall development expect to alleviate these emanations by advancing the utilization of elective materials, like fly debris or slag, to supplant concrete in concrete to some extent. Moreover, carbon offset techniques and the fuse of environmentally friendly power sources, like sunlight based chargers, further add to decreasing the carbon impression of mall development.

Water protection is an essential thought in green structure rehearses. Conventional building destinations frequently bring about soil disintegration, environment interruption, and expanded water overflow, which can adversely affect nearby biological systems. Practical development techniques focus on disintegration control measures, water collecting frameworks, and the utilization of penetrable surfaces to decrease water overflow and improve groundwater re-energize. By executing these actions, retail outlet development can limit its effect on nearby water assets.

The idea of green rooftops is acquiring unmistakable quality in economical retail outlet development. Green rooftops include the development of vegetation on the roof, giving protection, decreasing stormwater overflow, and alleviating the metropolitan intensity island impact. Incorporating green rooftops into retail plaza plan upgrades natural execution as well as adds to making stylishly satisfying and reasonable metropolitan scenes.

Squander the executives is a critical test in development, with significant measures of waste produced during destruction and building processes. Green structure rehearses focus on squander decrease through procedures like reusing, reusing materials, and limiting development squander. Development squander the executives plans are vital to maintainable retail plaza development, guaranteeing that materials are arranged and discarded mindfully.

Moreover, feasible development rehearses underscore the significance of ecologically mindful transportation. Conventional development projects frequently include broad transportation of materials and hardware, adding to air contamination and gridlock. Green structure rehearses empower the utilization of privately obtained materials to lessen transportation-related natural effects. Moreover, consolidating bicycle racks, passerby well disposed pathways, and public transportation availability in retail outlet plans advances eco-accommodating driving choices.

The development business' effect on biological systems and biodiversity is one more viewpoint tended to by green structure rehearses. Economical retail plaza development plans to limit environment disturbance, safeguard existing biological systems, and consolidate finishing that upholds neighborhood biodiversity. This might include protecting existing green spaces, establishing local vegetation, and executing supportable arranging rehearses that improve biological versatility.

Confirmations and norms assume a urgent part in directing green structure rehearses in mall development. Administration in Energy and Ecological Plan (LEED) affirmation is one of the most generally perceived principles for naturally manageable development. Retail plaza engineers and manufacturers frequently seek after LEED accreditation to exhibit their obligation to green structure rehearses and separate their ventures on the lookout.

Lifecycle evaluation is an exhaustive methodology utilized in green structure practices to assess the ecological effect of a structure from development through activity and possible destruction. This includes considering elements, for example, materials determination, energy use, water utilization, and waste age. By evaluating the whole lifecycle, retail outlet development can distinguish open doors for development and settle on informed choices that line up with maintainability objectives.

Furthermore, green structure rehearses in retail plaza development reach out to the domain of social obligation. Practical development projects focus on the prosperity of development laborers, guaranteeing safe working circumstances, fair wages, and admittance to conveniences. Social maintainability in development likewise includes drawing in with nearby networks, tending to worries, and cultivating positive connections all through the development cycle.

Joint effort and correspondence among partners are critical for the effective execution of green structure rehearses. This incorporates engineers, manufacturers, designers, inhabitants, and neighborhood specialists cooperating to adjust objectives, share information, and beat difficulties. Coordinated plan draws near, where different disciplines work together from the undertaking's beginning, improve the probability of accomplishing maintainability targets in retail plaza development.

All in all, green structure rehearses in retail plaza development address an extraordinary way to deal with address natural difficulties and advance economical turn of events. By focusing on eco-accommodating materials, energy productivity, water protection, squander decrease, and social obligation, supportable mall development means to make spaces that contribute decidedly to the climate and encompassing networks. As the interest for manageability keeps on developing, the reception of green structure rehearses becomes a dependable decision as well as a critical differentiator in the serious scene of retail outlet improvement. Through development, coordinated effort, and a pledge to long haul natural stewardship, the development business can assume an essential part in forming an additional economical and versatile future.

## 6.2 Sustainable operations and energy efficiency

Maintainable tasks and energy productivity are basic parts of dependable strategic policies, pivotal in tending to natural difficulties and advancing a more practical future. In different ventures, including assembling, transportation, and administrations, the manner in which organizations work and use energy essentially influences their biological impression. This is especially applicable with regards to worldwide endeavors to battle environmental change and lessen ozone depleting substance outflows.

One critical part of reasonable activities is the proficient utilization of energy assets. Energy utilization is a significant supporter of ecological corruption, principally through the consuming of petroleum derivatives. Organizations can take on reasonable energy rehearses by executing energy-proficient advances, upgrading functional cycles, and embracing sustainable power sources. These actions lessen the ecological effect as well as add to cost reserve funds and long haul flexibility.

The execution of energy-proficient innovations is a foundation of economical tasks. Organizations can put resources into energy-proficient apparatuses, lighting frameworks, and hardware to decrease generally energy utilization. For example, the reception of Driven lighting, which consumes fundamentally less energy than customary lighting, is a basic yet powerful way for organizations to upgrade energy productivity. Moreover, cutting edge innovations, for example, brilliant sensors and mechanization frameworks can advance energy use by changing utilization in light of constant interest.

Environmentally friendly power sources assume a urgent part in manageable tasks, offering a cleaner and more reasonable option in contrast to customary petroleum products. Sun powered, wind, hydro, and geothermal energy are among the inexhaustible choices accessible to organizations. Introducing sun powered chargers on housetops, tackling wind energy, or using geothermal warming and cooling frameworks are instances of how organizations can change towards a more economical energy blend. Such drives diminish the carbon impression as well as add to building a strong and decentralized energy framework.

Energy reviews are fundamental apparatuses for organizations to survey their energy utilization designs, recognize shortcomings, and execute designated enhancements. By breaking down energy use across different tasks, organizations can pinpoint regions where energy effectiveness measures can be executed. This might incorporate updating hardware, further developing protection, and advancing warming, ventilation, and cooling (central air) frameworks. Energy reviews give a guide to organizations to upgrade maintainability by diminishing waste and working on generally functional productivity.

In the domain of assembling, reasonable activities frequently include upgrading creation cycles to limit energy utilization and waste age. Lean assembling standards, which center around wiping out failures and lessening waste, line up with supportability objectives. Organizations can embrace practices like without a moment to spare creation, reusing of materials, and the utilization of harmless to the ecosystem producing strategies to work on their in general natural effect.

The transportation area assumes a huge part in maintainable tasks, especially concerning eco-friendliness and discharges decrease. Organizations with armadas of vehicles can embrace eco-friendly advances, like cross breed or electric vehicles, to limit their carbon impression.

Furthermore, streamlining transportation courses and executing operations techniques that focus on productivity add to both natural and financial manageability.

The idea of roundabout economy rehearses is getting some momentum in maintainable tasks. Rather than following a straight model of creation, utilization, and removal, the roundabout economy stresses lessening, reusing, and reusing materials. Organizations can execute round economy standards by planning items for life span, empowering the reuse of materials, and carrying out reusing programs. This approach limits squander as well as advances a more reasonable and regenerative way to deal with asset use.

Feasible store network the board is a basic thought in general business manageability. Organizations can evaluate the ecological effect of their stock chains and work towards obtaining materials mindfully. This incorporates choosing providers with solid ecological works on, advancing fair work conditions, and limiting the carbon impression related with the transportation of merchandise. Practical inventory network the executives guarantees that the whole lifecycle of an item is thought of, from natural substance extraction to end-of-life removal.

In the domain of structures and foundation, economical tasks include the execution of green structure rehearses. This incorporates planning and developing energy-proficient structures, using economical materials, and consolidating environmentally friendly power sources. Building robotization frameworks, which control lighting, warming, and cooling in view of inhabitance and outside conditions, add to energy productivity. Moreover, feasible structures frequently highlight green rooftops, water reaping frameworks, and proficient waste administration rehearses.

Water preservation is a fundamental part of supportable tasks, especially in locales confronting water shortage. Organizations can carry out water-productive advancements, for example, low-stream installations and water reusing frameworks, to limit water utilization. Reasonable arranging rehearses, for example, xeriscaping and water collecting for water system, further add to capable water the board. By focusing on water protection, organizations lessen their natural effect as well as add to the general strength of water assets.

Worker commitment is a significant figure the progress of feasible tasks. Organizations can encourage a culture of supportability by instructing representatives about the significance of energy productivity and mindful practices. Worker contribution in maintainability drives, from energy-saving rivalries to squander decrease programs, makes a feeling of aggregate liability. Moreover, organizations can boost maintainable practices, for example, carpooling or utilizing public transportation, to additionally advance a culture of natural stewardship.

Feasible tasks additionally reach out to the domain of data innovation (IT). Server farms, which are imperative parts of present day organizations, can be huge energy buyers. Organizations can carry out energy-proficient server farm plans, use virtualization advancements, and upgrade cooling frameworks to improve IT supportability.

Distributed computing, which considers shared assets and improved energy use, is one more road for organizations to diminish their IT-related natural effect.

Affirmations and norms give organizations systems for executing feasible tasks. Perceived confirmations, for example, ISO 14001 for ecological administration or ENERGY STAR for energy proficiency, exhibit a guarantee to feasible practices. Organizations can seek after significant certificates to feature their devotion to ecological obligation and separate themselves on the lookout.

All in all, reasonable activities and energy proficiency are crucial for organizations looking to flourish in a time of expanding natural mindfulness and obligation. By taking on energy-proficient innovations, embracing environmentally friendly power sources, streamlining processes, and participating in economical store network rehearses, organizations can lessen their natural effect and add to a more manageable future. The reconciliation of supportability into tasks isn't just a moral objective yet additionally a competitive edge, as shoppers and partners progressively esteem organizations that focus on natural obligation. As organizations keep on developing, the coordination of economical practices into everyday tasks turns into a major part of corporate achievement and a vital driver for a more feasible and tough worldwide economy.

### 6.3 Consumer preferences for eco-friendly shopping destinations

Buyer inclinations for eco-accommodating shopping objections have gone through a critical change as of late, mirroring a developing mindfulness and worry for natural manageability. As worldwide natural difficulties become more evident, buyers are progressively disposed to pursue earth cognizant decisions, including their choice of shopping objections. This change in customer conduct has provoked organizations, especially in the retail and land areas, to adjust and coordinate supportable practices into their tasks and framework.

One of the essential elements impacting customer inclinations for eco-accommodating shopping objections is an increased consciousness of natural issues. Issues, for example, environmental change, deforestation, and contamination stand out, driving customers to reconsider their buying propensities and the effect of their decisions in the world. Accordingly, buyers are looking for shopping objections that line up with their qualities and add to positive ecological results.

Eco-accommodating shopping objections focus on maintainability across different aspects of their activities, from the plan and development of actual spaces to the obtaining and bundling of items. Green structure rehearses, like energy-productive plans, the utilization of manageable materials, and eco-accommodating finishing, add to the general allure of shopping objections. Customers are progressively attracted to spaces that mirror a promise to limiting ecological effect and advancing dependable asset use.

Reasonable transportation choices likewise assume a critical part in customer inclinations for eco-accommodating shopping objections. Buyers value retail plazas that give helpful admittance to public transportation, bicycle racks, and person on foot agreeable pathways. Offering electric vehicle charging stations further improves the allure of a shopping objective, lining up with the rising reception of eco-accommodating transportation options among earth cognizant buyers.

The accessibility of eco-accommodating items is a critical consider impacting customer decisions shopping objections. Buyers effectively look for retailers and malls that focus on harmless to the ecosystem and morally obtained items. This change in shopper conduct has prompted a flood popular for eco-cognizant brands and organizations that exhibit a guarantee to maintainable obtaining, creation practices, and bundling.

Because of changing shopper inclinations, many shopping objections have executed manageability drives that reach out past the items they offer. This incorporates endeavors to decrease single-utilize plastic, energize reusing, and limit squander age. Eco-accommodating shopping objections frequently team up with retailers to execute eco-accommodating bundling arrangements, lessening the natural effect of item bundling and adding to a roundabout economy.

Training and mindfulness crusades inside shopping objections can likewise impact shopper inclinations. Reasonable retail outlets frequently take part in enlightening efforts that feature their eco-accommodating practices, exhibit earth cognizant brands, and give shoppers tips on settling on manageable decisions. By effectively advancing natural mindfulness, shopping objections can engage buyers to settle on informed choices that line up with their qualities.

The coordination of innovation in shopping objections adds to eco-accommodating practices and upgrades the general customer experience. For instance, savvy lighting and warming frameworks that change in view of inhabitance assist with lessening energy utilization. Computerized signage can pass on data about supportability drives, advancements on eco-accommodating items, and constant reports on energy-saving measures, cultivating a feeling of straightforwardness and commitment with buyers.

Purchaser inclinations for eco-accommodating shopping objections are additionally molded by the social obligation drives of organizations. Retail outlets that effectively take part in local area commitment, support neighborhood natural causes, and add to magnanimous drives show a promise to more extensive social and ecological qualities. Purchasers are bound to pick shopping objections that line up with their moral convictions and contribute emphatically to the networks they serve.

Certificates and guidelines for economical practices assume a urgent part in impacting buyer inclinations.

Shopping objections that accomplish perceived certificates, like LEED (Authority in Energy and Natural Plan) for green structure practices or certificates for supportable obtaining, convey a promise to satisfying explicit ecological guidelines. These accreditations act as signs of validity and straightforwardness, affecting shoppers who focus on earth dependable decisions.

The ascent of web based business and internet shopping has likewise influenced shopper inclinations for eco-accommodating shopping objections. While internet shopping offers comfort, customers are progressively worried about the ecological effect of bundling, transportation discharges, and the general manageability of the store network. This has prompted a restored appreciation for actual shopping objections that focus on supportability in both their tasks and the items they offer.

Buyer inclinations for eco-accommodating shopping objections are not restricted to explicit socioeconomics; rather, they range across different age gatherings and pay levels. Recent college grads and Age Z, specifically, have been distinguished as companions with serious areas of strength for an on maintainability in their buying choices. In any case, research shows that purchasers of any age are progressively considering natural variables while picking where to shop, flagging a more extensive change in cultural qualities.

The financial effect of purchaser inclinations for eco-accommodating shopping objections is imperative. As additional customers focus on maintainability, organizations that line up with these qualities stand to acquire an upper hand. Malls and retailers that proactively take on and advance eco-accommodating practices are probably going to draw in a bigger client base, prompting expanded people walking through, higher deals, and positive brand discernment.

Retailers inside eco-accommodating shopping objections can likewise assume a urgent part in forming shopper inclinations. By effectively advancing reasonable items, giving data on the natural effect of items, and integrating eco-accommodating practices into their activities, retailers add to the general manageability account of the shopping objective. Purchaser devotion is much of the time cultivated when retailers line up with the supportability upsides of their client base.

Purchaser inclinations for eco-accommodating shopping objections are dynamic and likely to advancing patterns and advancements. As manageability keeps on being a focal subject in cultural talk, organizations should remain receptive to changing purchaser assumptions and persistently reconsider and improve their eco-accommodating drives. This versatility is urgent for keeping up with buyer unwaveringness, remaining serious, and adding to more extensive ecological objectives.

All in all, customer inclinations for eco-accommodating shopping objections mirror a more extensive cultural shift towards supportability. As ecological mindfulness develops, customers progressively look for shopping objections that line up with their qualities and add to positive natural results. From green structure practices to maintainable transportation choices, the accessibility of eco-accommodating items, and local area commitment drives, shopping objections assume a vital part in molding and meeting purchaser assumptions for a more feasible and capable retail insight. The joining of eco-accommodating practices isn't just a reaction to shopper interest yet in addition an essential basic for organizations hoping to flourish in a period where maintainability is a focal thought in buyer navigation.

Eco-accommodating shopping objections have arisen as a reaction to expanding buyer mindfulness and interest for manageable and earth capable retail encounters. These objections, going from individual stores to whole retail plazas, focus on natural contemplations in their plan, activities, and item contributions. This change in the retail scene mirrors a more extensive cultural obligation to natural manageability, where customers are effectively looking for ways of limiting their environmental impression and backing organizations that share their qualities.

One of the critical highlights of eco-accommodating shopping objections is the combination of green structure rehearses. Supportable engineering and plan standards are utilized to make structures that limit ecological effect. This incorporates the utilization of eco-accommodating materials, energy-productive plans, and naturally cognizant finishing. Green rooftops, water gathering frameworks, and energy-effective lighting are normal elements in these spaces, exhibiting a pledge to lessening asset utilization and advancing ecological stewardship.

The area and openness of eco-accommodating shopping objections likewise assume a pivotal part in their general manageability. Closeness to public transportation, bicycle paths, and person on foot agreeable pathways supports harmless to the ecosystem methods of transportation. Malls that focus on simple admittance to public travel or give offices to cyclists not just diminish the carbon impression related with driving yet in addition advance a more maintainable way to deal with transportation.

Energy effectiveness is a foundation of eco-accommodating shopping objections. These objections embrace trend setting innovations and practices to limit energy utilization. Brilliant lighting frameworks, energy-productive central air (warming, ventilation, and cooling) frameworks, and the utilization of environmentally friendly power sources, like sunlight based chargers, add to the general energy effectiveness of these spaces. The objective isn't just to decrease functional expenses yet in addition to show a guarantee to reasonable practices and ecological obligation.

Squander decrease and dependable waste administration are vital parts of eco-accommodating shopping objections. These spaces effectively work to limit the age of waste and advance reusing drives. Reusing containers, fertilizing the soil offices, and instructive projects for customers on mindful garbage removal add to a culture of maintainability inside these objections. Some eco-accommodating retail outlets even carry out squander to-energy innovations to additionally lessen their natural effect.

Water protection is one more key part of eco-accommodating shopping objections. Supportable arranging rehearses, for example, xeriscaping and the utilization of local plants, lessen the requirement for over the top water utilization. Moreover, water-proficient apparatuses, water collecting frameworks, and the utilization of reused water for non-consumable purposes add to generally speaking water preservation endeavors. By executing these actions, eco-accommodating shopping objections expect to limit their effect on nearby water assets.

The item contributions inside eco-accommodating shopping objections mirror a pledge to manageability. Retailers in these spaces effectively source items that meet eco-accommodating standards, for example, being produced using reasonable materials, created utilizing earth cognizant practices, and bundled with negligible natural effect. The accentuation is on advancing morally obtained and ecologically capable items, offering customers the chance to pursue more supportable decisions in their buying choices.

Roundabout economy standards assume a huge part in molding the tasks of eco-accommodating shopping objections. As opposed to following a direct model of creation, utilization, and removal, these objections focus on diminishing, reusing, and reusing materials. Retailers inside eco-accommodating malls frequently partake in reclaim programs, support the reuse of materials, and investigate imaginative answers for limiting the natural effect of their items all through their lifecycle.

Innovation and advancement are utilized to improve the supportability of eco-accommodating shopping objections. Shrewd advances, like IoT (Web of Things) gadgets and information examination, empower more productive energy the board, squander observing, and by and large asset streamlining. These innovations not just add to the functional effectiveness of the shopping objections yet additionally give significant information to ceaseless improvement and the recognizable proof of new open doors for supportability.

Buyer instruction is an indispensable part of eco-accommodating shopping objections. These spaces effectively draw in with customers to bring issues to light about natural issues, advance supportable practices, and feature the eco-accommodating drives carried out inside the shopping objective. Instructive projects, signage, and computerized shows give data on practical living, dependable utilization, and the positive effect of going with eco-cognizant decisions.

Local area commitment is a critical concentration for eco-accommodating shopping objections. These spaces perceive their job in the neighborhood local area and effectively try to include occupants in their maintainability drives. This might incorporate getting sorted out local area occasions, joining forces with nearby ecological associations, and supporting drives that add to the general prosperity of the local area. By cultivating a feeling of shared liability, eco-accommodating shopping objections become necessary pieces of the networks they serve.

Confirmations and principles are significant marks of a shopping objective's obligation to supportability. Different associations offer affirmations for eco-accommodating structures, like LEED (Administration in Energy and Natural Plan). Accomplishing these confirmations shows a commitment to satisfying thorough natural guidelines and gives an unmistakable marker to customers looking for eco-accommodating shopping choices. Also, adherence to perceived principles upgrades the believability and straightforwardness of eco-accommodating shopping objections.

Eco-accommodating shopping objections effectively team up with retailers to intensify maintainability endeavors. They urge and boost retailers to embrace eco-accommodating practices, like diminishing bundling, carrying out reusing programs, and obtaining items capably. By cultivating a cooperative methodology, shopping objections make a brought together obligation to maintainability, guaranteeing that both the framework and the items inside the space add to by and large ecological objectives.

With regards to eco-accommodating shopping objections, the idea of "green renting" has acquired conspicuousness. Green renting includes arrangements among landowners and occupants that integrate supportability measures into rent terms. This might incorporate energy effectiveness guidelines, squander decrease objectives, and responsibilities to source ecologically capable items. Green renting adjusts the interests of property managers and occupants in accomplishing shared supportability targets.

Customer input and commitment are significant apparatuses for the consistent improvement of eco-accommodating shopping objections. Retail plazas effectively look for input from customers on their maintainability inclinations, accumulate criticism on carried out drives, and utilize this data to refine and improve their manageability methodologies. By staying receptive to customer inclinations, eco-accommodating shopping objections can develop and adjust to live up to the changing assumptions of earth cognizant customers.

Eco-accommodating shopping objections contribute not exclusively to natural supportability yet in addition to the monetary feasibility of the organizations working inside them. Purchasers progressively favor shopping objections that line up with their qualities, and organizations that exhibit a guarantee to manageability frequently appreciate expanded client dependability and positive brand discernment.

This positive connection among's maintainability and financial achievement boosts more organizations to take on eco-accommodating practices inside shopping objections.

All in all, eco-accommodating shopping objections address a proactive reaction to developing shopper inclinations and a guarantee to natural maintainability. By coordinating green structure rehearses, energy proficiency measures, squander decrease drives, and economical item contributions, these objections make spaces that mirror a devotion to mindful strategic policies. As buyer familiarity with natural issues keeps on developing, the job of eco-accommodating shopping objections turns out to be progressively huge in forming a more practical and principled retail scene. The continuous development of these objections will probably be impacted by progressions in innovation, changing purchaser assumptions, and the cooperative endeavors of organizations, retailers, and networks focused on a more practical future.

# Chapter 7

## Marketing and Branding

Showcasing and marking are basic parts of any business system, filling in as the main impetus behind an organization's prosperity. In the present exceptionally cutthroat and dynamic business scene, laying out major areas of strength for a presence is fundamental for acquiring an upper hand and encouraging client steadfastness. This broad investigation will dive into the complexities of advertising and marking, looking at their reliance, advancement over the long haul, and the basic job they play in forming purchaser discernments and driving business development.

**Characterizing Advertising and Marking**

At its center, showcasing includes the exercises an organization embraces to advance and sell its items or administrations. It includes understanding client needs and inclinations, creating items that address those issues, deciding the right valuing methodology, and making viable channels for circulation. Showcasing is a diverse discipline that consolidates different components, including promoting, advertising, deals advancements, and statistical surveying.

Marking, then again, is the most common way of making and dealing with a brand - an interesting personality that recognizes an organization and its items or administrations from contenders. A brand is something other than a logo; it includes the general insight and encounters related with an organization. Fruitful marking makes a close to home association with buyers, encouraging trust and unwaveringness.

**The Development of Advertising and Marking**

The scene of showcasing and marking has gone through huge changes throughout the long term, molded by mechanical headways, changes in customer conduct, and changes in worldwide business sectors. Conventional showcasing techniques, for example, print publicizing and TV ads, have given way to computerized promoting methodologies, including web-based entertainment crusades, powerhouse advertising, and site improvement.

In the advanced age, buyers are more enabled and informed than any other time. They approach an abundance of data readily available, permitting them to explore items, read surveys, and settle on informed buying choices. This shift has required a more customized and client driven way to deal with showcasing and marking.

Furthermore, the ascent of virtual entertainment has generally modified the manner in which brands associate with their crowd. Stages like Facebook, Instagram, and Twitter furnish organizations with direct channels to draw in with shoppers, accumulate criticism, and construct networks around their brands. Virtual entertainment likewise enhances the effect of verbal exchange promoting, as fulfilled clients share their encounters with a more extensive crowd.

### The Interconnectedness of Showcasing and Marking

While showcasing and marking are particular disciplines, they are innately interconnected. Promoting exercises add to building and supporting a brand's character, and a solid brand upgrades the viability of showcasing endeavors. The connection among promoting and marking is advantageous, with each affecting and molding the other.

Powerful promoting efforts can lift brand mindfulness and make positive relationship in the personalities of shoppers. On the other hand, a deeply grounded brand can put forth promoting attempts more significant by giving a strong groundwork to informing and correspondence. The collaboration among promoting and marking is obvious in fruitful organizations that consistently coordinate the two viewpoints into their general business system.

### Building Serious areas of strength for a Character

Making serious areas of strength for a character is a foundation of effective marking. A brand personality envelops the visual components, informing, and values that characterize how an organization introduces itself to the world. This incorporates the logo, variety range, typography, and other plan components that add to a firm and conspicuous brand picture.

Consistency is key while building a brand personality. Whether a buyer experiences a brand via web-based entertainment, a site, or an actual store, the informing and visual components ought to adjust to make a bound together brand insight. This consistency fabricates trust and builds up the brand's personality in the personalities of shoppers.

Past visual components, a brand's voice and tone assume a urgent part in molding its character. The language utilized in promoting materials, web-based entertainment posts, and client correspondences ought to mirror the brand's character and reverberate with its ideal interest group. This consistency in correspondence reinforces the profound association between the brand and its shoppers.

### The Job of Narrating in Marking

Narrating has arisen as an amazing asset in marking, permitting organizations to associate with purchasers on a more profound level. A convincing brand story goes past item elements and features the organization's qualities, mission, and the effect it means to make on the planet. This story draws in purchasers inwardly, making an essential and significant association.

Fruitful brand stories frequently consolidate the excursion of the organization, its pioneers, or individuals behind the brand. Sharing genuine and engaging stories adapts the brand, making it more interesting to customers. In a time where validness is profoundly esteemed, narrating gives an approach to brands to stick out and fabricate veritable associations with their crowd.

**Shopper Insight and Brand Value**

Shopper discernment assumes a crucial part in forming a brand's prosperity. What customers see a brand means for their buying choices, brand steadfastness, and support. Brand value, a proportion of a brand's worth and strength, is intently attached to customer insight.

Positive customer discernment is worked through steady conveyance of value items or administrations, straightforward correspondence, and paramount brand encounters. Brands with high value are many times tough notwithstanding challenges, as buyers are really lenient and steady of brands they trust.

Brand value likewise stretches out to immaterial resources like brand notoriety and altruism. A positive standing worked over the long run can be a critical upper hand, as purchasers are bound to pick brands they see emphatically, regardless of whether they are valued higher than choices.

**The Effect of Innovation on Showcasing and Marking**

Progressions in innovation have altered the showcasing and marking scene, offering new roads for coming to and connecting with purchasers. Computerized advertising devices and stages empower exceptionally focused on and customized crusades, permitting organizations to fit their informing to explicit socioeconomics.

Information investigation and man-made consciousness (simulated intelligence) have become essential parts of current showcasing systems. These advances empower organizations to assemble and dissect tremendous measures of information, acquiring experiences into customer conduct, inclinations, and patterns. This information driven approach upgrades the adequacy of advertising efforts, taking into account continuous changes in view of buyer reactions.

In the domain of marking, innovation has worked with intelligent and vivid brand encounters. Computer generated reality (VR) and expanded reality (AR) applications permit purchasers to draw in with brands in creative ways, for example, virtual item exhibitions or intelligent brand narrating encounters. These innovations make critical and shareable minutes that add to a brand's general personality.

**Difficulties and Open doors in Promoting and Marking**

While innovation has opened additional opportunities, it has likewise introduced difficulties for advertisers and brand tacticians. The computerized scene is immersed with content, making it trying for brands to catch and hold buyer consideration.

Adjusting to quickly changing innovation patterns and buyer conduct requires readiness and an eagerness to embrace development.

One huge test is dealing with a brand's web-based standing in the time of virtual entertainment. Negative surveys and remarks can immediately spread, affecting shopper insight. Organizations must proactively screen and address online input to safeguard and improve their image picture.

Be that as it may, challenges likewise bring open doors. Online entertainment, for instance, gives a stage to coordinate commitment with buyers, permitting brands to address concerns, exhibit positive encounters, and construct a local area around their items or administrations. Utilizing web-based entertainment as a device for client care and relationship-building is a vital chance for brands to separate themselves on the lookout.

**Moral Contemplations in Advertising and Marking**

As brands explore the intricacies of the cutting edge business scene, moral contemplations have become progressively significant. Shoppers are more aware of the qualities and practices of the organizations they support, and dishonest way of behaving can prompt reputational harm and loss of trust.

Moral promoting includes straightforward and legitimate correspondence with shoppers. This incorporates exact item data, fair estimating rehearses, and capable publicizing. Brands that focus on moral conduct in their promoting and marking endeavors construct trust as well as add to a positive brand picture.

Manageability has likewise turned into a point of convergence in marking, with purchasers putting a superior on harmless to the ecosystem and socially mindful brands. Organizations that embrace feasible practices and convey their obligation to social and ecological obligation can engage a developing section of cognizant buyers.

**Globalization and Social Contemplations**

In a period of globalization, marks frequently work on a worldwide scale, contacting different crowds with fluctuated social foundations. Social contemplations are critical in both promoting and marking, as social subtleties can essentially affect how a brand is seen.

Adjusting promoting systems to various social settings requires a profound comprehension of neighborhood customs, values, and inclinations. Brands should be delicate to social variety and keep away from methodologies that might be seen as heartless or improper in unambiguous areas.

Essentially, building a worldwide brand requires a nuanced way to deal with marking that rises above social limits. A brand's basic beliefs and informing ought to resound with a different crowd while considering social customization when fundamental. Fruitful worldwide brands work out some kind of harmony between keeping a predictable brand character and adjusting to neighborhood social subtleties.

**Arising Patterns in Advertising and Marking**

The scene of advertising and marking keeps on developing, driven by innovative headways, moving shopper conduct, and arising patterns. A few remarkable patterns forming the fate of promoting and marking include:

**Powerhouse Promoting:** Teaming up with forces to be reckoned with has turned into a noticeable methodology for brands to reach and draw in with their interest group. Powerhouses, who have laid out believability and a critical continuing in unambiguous specialties, can genuinely elevate items or administrations to their crowd.

**Transient Substance:** The ascent of fleeting substance on stages like Instagram and Snapchat has meaningfully impacted the manner in which brands approach narrating. Impermanent and vanishing content makes a need to keep moving and legitimacy, empowering constant commitment.

**Personalization and artificial intelligence:** Customized promoting encounters, filled by simulated intelligence and information investigation, empower brands to fit their informing and contributions to individual buyer inclinations. From customized item proposals to modified email crusades, personalization upgrades the general client experience.

**Reason Driven Promoting:** Customers progressively support marks that line up with their qualities and add to social or natural causes. Reason driven showcasing includes imparting a brand's obligation to having a constructive outcome, past selling items or administrations.

**Voice Inquiry Advancement:** With the ascent of menial helpers and brilliant speakers, enhancing content for voice search is becoming urgent. Brands need to adjust their computerized presence to oblige voice-enacted search questions and give applicable data.

**Intuitive Substance:** Intuitive substance, for example, tests, surveys, and studies, draws in crowds such that customary substance can't. This pattern permits brands to accumulate important information while giving an agreeable and intuitive experience for purchasers.

**Expanded Reality (AR) Shopping Encounters:** AR is overall progressively coordinated into web based business stages, permitting customers to take a stab at items prior to making a buy for all intents and purposes. This vivid experience upgrades the web based shopping process and lessens vulnerabilities about item appropriateness.

### 7.1 Creating a strong brand identity for shopping centers

Making areas of strength for a personality for retail plazas is a multi-layered and vital undertaking that includes a far reaching comprehension of the market, customer conduct, and the exceptional properties of the actual mall. A very much created brand personality goes past a logo or signage; it embodies the substance of the mall, making a critical and significant association with guests. This investigation dives into the vital parts of building a hearty brand personality for retail plazas, looking at the significance of separation, experiential plan, local area commitment, and computerized presence.

**Grasping the Market and Interest group**

Prior to setting out on the excursion to make a brand character, it is pivotal to direct an exhaustive investigation of the market and recognize the ideal interest group. Malls take care of assorted shopper sections, each with its inclinations, ways of behaving, and assumptions. Figuring out the socioeconomics, psychographics, and shopping propensities for the neighborhood local area is basic to fitting the brand character to reverberate with the ideal interest group.

Statistical surveying gives bits of knowledge into the serious scene, permitting malls to recognize novel selling focuses and regions for separation. By understanding the requirements and wants of the objective segment, a mall can situate itself decisively, offering an unmistakable encounter that separates it from contenders.

**Separation and Situating**

In a soaked market, separation is the foundation of a solid brand character. Malls should distinguish and verbalize what makes them interesting, whether it's the blend of retailers, the atmosphere, unique occasions, or conveniences. The brand situating ought to impart the incentive, underscoring the justifications for why purchasers ought to pick a specific retail plaza over others.

Viable separation requires a profound comprehension of the main interest group's inclinations and yearnings. For instance, a retail plaza situated as a family-accommodating location might zero in on offering diversion choices for youngsters, while an extravagance mall could underscore select brands and upscale encounters. By adjusting the brand to the cravings and ways of life of the interest group, a mall can make a convincing and separated personality.

**Experiential Plan and Environment**

The actual climate of a retail outlet assumes a urgent part in molding the general brand insight. Experiential plan goes past feel; it includes making an environment that connects with the faculties, brings out feelings, and supports delayed visits. The design, engineering, lighting, and finishing add to the general feel and ought to line up with the ideal brand picture.

A cautiously organized blend of stores, eateries, and diversion choices upgrades the experiential part of a retail plaza. Insightful plan components, like happy with seating regions, intelligent establishments, and craftsmanship establishments, add to an inviting and pleasant climate. The objective is to change the mall into something beyond a retail space yet an objective where guests can mingle, unwind, and make positive recollections.

**Marking Through Visual Character**

The visual character is a substantial articulation of a mall's image. This incorporates the logo, variety range, typography, and by and large plan stylish. An outwardly durable character builds up memorability and establishes the vibe for the buyer experience. The visual components ought to line up with the brand's character and resound with the ideal interest group.

The logo, as a focal part of the visual character, ought to be unmistakable and critical. It fills in as an obvious prompt that addresses the substance of the mall. The variety range adds to the general state of mind, with each tone conveying its own mental affiliations. Typography, when picked nicely, adds to the brand's personality and clarity.

Consistency in visual marking across different touchpoints, from signage to promoting guarantee, is fundamental for building serious areas of strength for a conspicuous brand. The visual character ought to be versatile to various organizations and mediums while keeping a brought together and strong look.

**Making a Feeling of Local area**

Malls can possibly become lively local area centers, and encouraging a feeling of local area is a strong part of brand character. Past a spot to shop, an effective retail plaza turns into a get-together space where individuals associate, mingle, and take part in shared encounters. This feeling of local area improves the close to home association guests have with the retail outlet.

Local area commitment drives, like neighborhood occasions, organizations with nearby organizations, and backing for worthy missions, add to building a positive local area picture. A retail outlet that effectively partakes in and adds to the nearby local area is bound to be embraced and upheld by occupants. This positive feeling stretches out to the brand character, supporting that the mall is a vital piece of the local area texture.

**Computerized Presence and Omnichannel Experience**

In the computerized age, a retail outlet's image stretches out past its actual space to the web-based domain. A hearty computerized presence is fundamental for coming to and drawing in with buyers previously, during, and after their visits. The retail outlet's site, virtual entertainment profiles, and internet showcasing endeavors ought to adjust flawlessly with its general image personality.

The site fills in as a virtual retail facade, giving data about stores, advancements, occasions, and conveniences. An easy to use and outwardly engaging site upgrades the general brand insight. Online entertainment stages offer open doors for continuous commitment, local area building, and displaying the character of the mall.

An omnichannel approach guarantees consistency across all shopper touchpoints, whether on the web or disconnected. This incorporates coordinating advanced innovations inside the actual space, for example, intuitive booths, versatile applications, and computerized signage. These advancements upgrade the shopping experience as well as add to the general brand way of life as imaginative and client driven.

**Integrating Brand Narrating**

Brand narrating is an incredible asset for conveying the qualities, history, and character of a retail plaza. The account goes past special substance to share the story behind the brand - its beginnings, development, and the effect it expects to make locally. Brand narrating makes a profound association with purchasers, cultivating a more profound comprehension of the retail outlet's personality.

The narrating account can feature key perspectives, for example, the improvement interaction, associations with neighborhood organizations, or the vision for what's to come. Realness is vital in brand narrating, and the story ought to reverberate with the upsides of the interest group.

Integrating narrating into promoting materials, both on the web and disconnected, adds profundity to the brand personality and furnishes buyers with a convincing motivation to draw in with the retail plaza.

**Estimating and Adjusting the Brand Personality**

Making areas of strength for a character is a continuous cycle that requires normal assessment and transformation. Estimating the adequacy of the brand character includes gathering criticism from guests, observing web-based entertainment opinions, and examining key execution markers (KPIs) connected with pedestrian activity, deals, and consumer loyalty.

Shopper criticism gives significant experiences into how the brand is seen and whether it lines up with the expected picture. Checking virtual entertainment permits the retail plaza to address concerns, celebrate positive encounters, and effectively take part in web-based discussions. KPIs give quantitative information on the effect of the brand character on key business measurements.

In view of the criticism and information gathered, retail outlets can adjust their image personality to more readily meet the developing requirements and inclinations of customers. This might include tweaking visual components, refining informing, or presenting new drives that line up with the brand's guiding principle. Adaptability and a readiness to develop are key characteristics of fruitful brand the executives.

**Contextual analyses in Fruitful Retail plaza Marking**

Looking at contextual analyses of effective retail outlet marking gives viable bits of knowledge into the procedures and strategies utilized by industry pioneers. Eminent models include:

**The Woods, Los Angeles:** The Woods is prestigious for its vivid and bubbly environment. The retail outlet's image personality stresses an extravagant yet open insight, with carefully planned public spaces, live diversion, and an organized choice of very good quality and well known brands. The visual personality mirrors an immortal and upscale stylish, while local area occasions and organizations add to major areas of strength for an of having a place.

**Chadstone Mall, Melbourne:** Known as the Design Capital, Chadstone is the biggest retail outlet in the Southern Side of the equator. Its image character revolves around extravagance, style, and a promise to giving an elite shopping experience. The visual character is smooth and refined, mirroring the very good quality retail contributions. Chadstone effectively draws in with the local area through style occasions, joint efforts with global fashioners, and a solid computerized presence.

**Shopping center of America, Minnesota:** As one of the biggest shopping and diversion edifices internationally, the Shopping center of America positions itself as an objective for shopping, feasting, and family-accommodating encounters.

The brand personality stresses the variety of contributions, from retail to event congregation attractions. The visual personality is lively and dynamic, mirroring the fiery air inside the shopping center. Local area commitment is encouraged through occasions, organizations, and a solid internet based presence.

These contextual investigations feature the different ways to deal with retail outlet marking, featuring the significance of adjusting the brand personality to the interesting attributes of the middle and its interest group.

Making major areas of strength for a personality for malls requires an essential mix of market grasping, separation, experiential plan, local area commitment, and a strong computerized presence. A fruitful brand character goes past feel, epitomizing the quintessence of the retail outlet and encouraging a close to home association with guests.

Separation is key in a serious market, and malls should distinguish and impart their novel selling focuses. Experiential plan improves the climate and changes the mall into an objective instead of simply a spot to shop. The visual personality, including the logo and in general plan stylish, ought to be outwardly strong and resound with the interest group.

Encouraging a feeling of local area adds to a good brand picture, situating the retail plaza as a necessary piece of the neighborhood texture. A solid computerized presence, including an easy to understand site and dynamic online entertainment commitment, expands the brand past the actual space. Brand narrating adds profundity to the character, sharing the story behind the retail plaza and making an account that reverberates with purchasers.

Estimating the viability of the brand personality through input, web-based entertainment observing, and key execution markers permits retail plazas to adjust and develop. Adaptability and a guarantee to continuous improvement are pivotal for keeping a significant and resounding brand character.

In the unique scene of retail outlet marking, fruitful models like The Woods, Chadstone Retail plaza, and Shopping center of America give significant bits of knowledge into the systems that drive buyer commitment and steadfastness. As malls keep on developing, a key and first rate brand personality will stay a foundation of progress, molding the general insight for guests and adding to the life span and significance of the middle on the lookout.

### 7.2 Marketing strategies to attract shoppers and tenants

Creating compelling showcasing techniques to draw in the two customers and occupants is a basic endeavor for malls expecting to flourish in a serious retail scene. The progress of a mall depends on its capacity to establish an energetic and engaging climate that attracts purchasers and captivates a different scope of inhabitants.

This investigation dives into key promoting procedures custom-made to draw in the two customers and occupants, underlining the significance of separation, local area commitment, computerized showcasing, and the making of a convincing generally speaking experience.

**Separation as a Vital Technique**

In a commercial center immersed with shopping choices, separation is principal to sticking out and drawing in the two customers and occupants. Retail plazas should recognize novel selling focuses that put them aside from contenders. This could incorporate an unmistakable blend of retailers, an emphasis on experiential contributions, or particular administrations that take care of explicit purchaser needs.

Understanding the ideal interest group is urgent for compelling separation. Fitting the retail outlet's contributions to meet the inclinations and desires of the neighborhood local area upgrades its allure. Separation can likewise be accomplished through imaginative occupant determination, consolidating a blend of notable brands, neighborhood organizations, and specialty retailers to make a different and connecting retail scene.

**Local area Commitment for Customer Fascination**

Building serious areas of strength for a with the neighborhood local area is a strong procedure for drawing in customers. Local area commitment drives make a feeling of having a place and add to the general allure of the mall. Occasions, like nearby business sectors, celebrations, and social festivals, unite individuals and upgrade the retail outlet's standing as a local area center point.

Joint efforts with neighborhood organizations and associations reinforce attaches with the local area. Facilitating noble cause occasions, cooperating with schools, or supporting nearby causes add to everyone's benefit as well as cultivate positive insights among customers. While the mall turns into a functioning member locally, it turns out to be something other than a retail objective — it turns into where individuals accumulate and interface.

**Advanced Showcasing for Customer Fascination**

In the computerized age, a powerful web-based presence is fundamental for drawing in customers. Computerized showcasing procedures envelop different channels, each filling a novel need in coming to and connecting with the interest group.

**Web-based Entertainment Showcasing:** Stages like Facebook, Instagram, and Twitter give chances to coordinate commitment with customers. Standard updates about advancements, occasions, and new store openings keep the crowd educated and energized. Connecting with content, like in the background glimpses, client tributes, and intuitive surveys, makes a dynamic and engaging web-based presence.

**Site design improvement (Web optimization):** Streamlining the mall's site for web crawlers guarantees perceivability when potential customers are searching for nearby retail objections. This incorporates utilizing applicable watchwords, making great substance, and it is versatile to guarantee that the site.

**Email Showcasing:** Building an information base of customers and sending designated email missions can be a powerful method for conveying advancements, elite offers, and impending occasions. Customized and pertinent substance improves the probability of customer commitment.

**Powerhouse Coordinated efforts:** Banding together with neighborhood forces to be reckoned with or bloggers can enhance the retail outlet's scope. Powerhouses frequently have a devoted following and can give genuine and engaging substance that reverberates with their crowd.

**Geo-designated Promoting:** Using geo-focusing on highlights in advanced publicizing permits the retail outlet to arrive at customers in unambiguous geographic areas. This is especially valuable for advancing time-touchy offers and occasions.

**Online Audits and Evaluations:** Empowering positive web-based surveys and dealing with the mall's web-based standing is indispensable. Customers frequently depend on surveys to go with informed choices, and a positive internet based presence can impact their discernments.

### Making a Convincing Shopping Experience

Past conventional promoting endeavors, the general shopping experience assumes a urgent part in drawing in and holding customers. A positive and paramount experience cultivates reliability and empowers rehash visits. Key parts of making a convincing shopping experience include:

**Visual Promoting:** The introduction of retail facades and shows essentially influences the general feeling of the mall. Well-organized and outwardly engaging showcases catch the consideration of customers and add to a positive air.

**Conveniences and Offices:** Offering helpful conveniences, like happy with seating regions, clean bathrooms, and family-accommodating spaces, upgrades the general insight. Customers are bound to invest energy and investigate the middle when their fundamental necessities are met.

**Occasions and Amusement:** Facilitating occasions, live exhibitions, and intuitive exercises add a component of energy to the shopping experience. Whether it's a style show, unrecorded music, or occasional festivals, occasions make a dynamic and connecting with air.

**Innovation Reconciliation:** Embracing innovation, for example, intuitive booths, portable applications, and contactless installment choices, upgrades comfort for customers. Innovation can likewise be utilized to give customized proposals, reliability programs, and virtual encounters.

**Client support Greatness:** Extraordinary client care has an enduring impact on customers. Thoroughly prepared and polite staff individuals add to a positive generally experience and urge customers to return.

**Maintainability Drives:** As natural awareness develops, coordinating manageability drives into the shopping experience can draw in eco-cognizant customers. This might incorporate reusing programs, energy-productive practices, or associations with manageable brands.

**Inhabitant Fascination Methodologies**

Drawing in a different scope of occupants is crucial for the outcome of a retail outlet. The occupant blend adds to the general allure and decides the middle's situating on the lookout. Procedures for drawing in occupants include:

**Designated Inhabitant Determination:** Understanding the inclinations of the objective segment permits malls to organize an occupant blend that resounds with neighborhood purchasers. This could include a mix of notable brands, one of a kind shops, and specialty stores that take care of explicit interests.

**Adaptable Renting Choices:** Offering adaptable renting game plans, like transient spring up spaces or pivoting booths, draws in various occupants, including arising brands and neighborhood business people. This adaptability permits the mall to adjust to changing purchaser patterns and keep the retail scene dynamic.

**Motivations and Backing Projects:** Giving impetuses, like diminished lease during the underlying lease time frame or help with advertising endeavors, urges inhabitants to pick the retail plaza as their area. Support projects can remember direction for store design, promoting, and advertising systems.

**Designated Showcasing to Inhabitants:** Exhibiting a guarantee to supporting occupants' prosperity through designated promoting endeavors can be a convincing component. Featuring the mall's obligation to elevating and directing people to individual stores cultivates a cooperative relationship.

**Working with Joint effort Among Occupants:** Empowering cooperation and cross-advancement among inhabitants makes a feeling of brotherhood and upgrades the general shopping experience. This could incorporate joint occasions, co-marked advancements, or shared faithfulness programs.

**Figuring out Occupant Needs:** Standard correspondence with existing occupants and understanding their necessities helps in refining the occupant blend. Adaptability to adjust and oblige changes in view of developing business sector patterns and occupant inclinations is vital for long haul achievement.

**Computerized Advertising for Inhabitant Fascination**

Computerized advertising isn't just instrumental in drawing in customers yet additionally in exhibiting the retail plaza as an alluring area for possible occupants. A solid web-based presence and designated computerized promoting systems can upgrade the perceivability of the mall among organizations searching for retail spaces. Strategies include:

**Committed Renting Site:** Having a devoted segment on the retail outlet's site for renting data gives an effectively open asset to possible inhabitants. This segment can incorporate insights concerning accessible spaces, renting choices, and the advantages of being important for the retail plaza.

**Advanced Handouts and Guarantee:** Making computerized leaflets and limited time materials that feature the upsides of renting space in the mall can be imparted to likely occupants. These materials can be dispersed through email crusades or made accessible on the renting site.

**Web-based Entertainment Promoting for Occupant Enrollment:** Designated online entertainment publicizing can contact a more extensive crowd of likely inhabitants. Supported posts displaying the advantages of being important for the mall, for example, high people strolling through, a different customer segment, and local area commitment drives, can draw in organizations looking for an ideal place.

**Email Missions to Organizations:** Creating designated email crusades coordinated at organizations searching for retail space permits the mall to straightforwardly impart renting potential open doors, benefits, and the general allure of turning into an inhabitant.

**Virtual Visits and Representations:** Using innovation to give virtual visits and perceptions of accessible spaces permits possible inhabitants to imagine their business inside the retail outlet. This can be especially compelling for drawing in organizations from outside the neighborhood.

### Observing and Adjusting Methodologies

Observing the viability of showcasing procedures is fundamental for ceaseless improvement. Both customer and occupant fascination endeavors ought to be routinely assessed through a mix of quantitative and subjective measures.

**People strolling through and Deals Measurements:** Following pedestrian activity examples and deals measurements gives important experiences into the progress of customer fascination methodologies. Understanding busy times, famous regions inside the retail outlet, and the relationship between's advertising endeavors and deals execution takes into account information driven independent direction.

**Customer Overviews and Criticism:** Direct input from customers, gathered through reviews or input structures, offers subjective bits of knowledge into their encounters. Understanding customer inclinations, fulfillment levels, and regions for development guides future advertising systems.

**Occupant Degrees of consistency and Fulfillment Studies:** Evaluating occupant standards for dependability and leading fulfillment reviews among existing inhabitants helps in grasping the viability of inhabitant fascination methodologies. High inhabitant fulfillment is in many cases demonstrative of a fruitful renting climate.

**Web-based Entertainment Investigation and Online Audits:** Checking virtual entertainment examination, including commitment measurements and opinion examination, gives bits of knowledge into the adequacy of computerized promoting endeavors. Online surveys and evaluations offer a subjective viewpoint on how customers see the retail plaza.

**Contender Examination:** Routinely assessing the systems utilized by contenders gives setting to the mall's exhibition. Understanding industry patterns, arising purchaser ways of behaving, and effective strategies utilized by other retail outlets can illuminate variation systems.

**Flexibility is pivotal in the powerful retail scene.** Systems that demonstrate fruitful ought to be supported, while those that yield poor outcomes ought to be reexamined and changed. Adaptability permits retail plazas to remain receptive to changing economic situations, arising patterns, and developing shopper inclinations.

## 7.3 The role of social media and digital marketing in promoting shopping centers

In the contemporary retail scene, the job of virtual entertainment and computerized showcasing is principal in advancing malls and making a dynamic, connecting with presence in the personalities of shoppers. These stages have become necessary parts of promoting methodologies, giving an immediate channel to correspondence, local area building, and the spread of designated content. This investigation dives into the diverse job of online entertainment and advanced advertising in the advancement of malls, tending to key angles like local area commitment, content procedure, powerhouse organizations, and the mix of innovation.

**Local area Commitment through Virtual Entertainment**

One of the essential jobs of virtual entertainment in advancing retail outlets is cultivating local area commitment. Social stages act as computerized centers where customers can interface with the retail plaza, different guests, and the neighborhood local area. Laying out a functioning and energetic internet based local area improves the general brand picture and adds to a positive impression of the mall.

**Virtual Entertainment Stages:** Using famous stages like Facebook, Instagram, Twitter, and Pinterest permits retail plazas to contact a different crowd. Every stage offers exceptional highlights that can be decisively utilized to connect with various socioeconomics.

**Normal Updates and Declarations:** Posting standard updates about advancements, occasions, new store openings, and other applicable data keeps the crowd educated and energized. Reliable correspondence supports the retail outlet's presence and energizes progressing commitment.

**Client Produced Content:** Empowering customers to share their encounters through client created content, for example, photographs, surveys, and tributes, gives real points of view as well as makes a feeling of local area. Reposting client produced content recognizes and praises the different local area of customers.

**Surveys and Reviews:** Gathering information and overviews via online entertainment permits retail outlets to assemble bits of knowledge into customer inclinations, conclusions, and assumptions. This intelligent methodology causes customers to feel appreciated and esteemed, cultivating a two-way correspondence channel.

**Occasion Advancement:** Online entertainment stages are amazing assets for advancing occasions facilitated by the retail plaza. Live inclusion, in the background impressions, and ongoing updates make expectation and drive participation.

**Vital Substance Improvement**

A pivotal part of computerized showcasing for malls is the improvement of vital substance that resounds with the interest group. The substance methodology ought to line up with the retail outlet's image personality, impart its remarkable offering focuses, and offer some benefit to the crowd.

**Visual Substance:** Given the visual idea of shopping, serious areas of strength for an on excellent visual substance is fundamental. This incorporates expertly shot photos, drawing in recordings, and outwardly engaging designs. Visual substance should exhibit the mall's feeling, the variety of stores, and the general insight.

**Occasional Missions:** Making themed crusades lined up with seasons, occasions, or nearby occasions keeps the substance new and significant. Occasional advancements, improvements, and occasions can be featured through computerized showcasing to drive traffic and make a need to get a move on.

**Narrating:** Consolidating narrating into content acculturates the retail outlet. Sharing tales about individuals behind the stores, the improvement of the middle, or its effect on the local area adds profundity and realness to the brand.

**Instructive Substance:** Giving instructive substance, for example, design tips, way of life guides, or item surveys, positions the retail outlet as an important asset for customers. Instructive substance improves the shopping experience and lays out the middle as an expert in its specialty.

**Intuitive Substance:** Intelligent substance, for example, tests, surveys, and difficulties, supports dynamic cooperation from the crowd. This kind of happy engages as well as increments commitment and supports sharing.

**Powerhouse Associations for Significant Advancement**

Teaming up with powerhouses has turned into a strong methodology for retail outlets to broaden their range, construct believability, and make valid associations with their interest group. Powerhouses, who have laid out trust and believability inside unambiguous specialties, can intensify the retail plaza's message and draw in new guests.

**Distinguishing Applicable Powerhouses:** Picking forces to be reckoned with whose content lines up with the retail outlet's image and interest group is pivotal. Whether they spend significant time in design, way of life, or neighborhood encounters, powerhouses ought to have a certified association with the local area.

**Powerhouse Takeovers:** Permitting powerhouses to assume control over the mall's virtual entertainment represents a day or during exceptional occasions gives a new point of view. It acquaints the powerhouse's supporters with the retail outlet and makes a buzz around their visit.

**Cooperative Substance:** Working together with powerhouses on satisfied creation, like supported posts, audits, or included stories, incorporates the mall into the powerhouse's account. Valid and engaging substance reverberates with the powerhouse's crowd.

**Occasion Cooperation:** Welcoming powerhouses to partake in mall occasions, dispatches, or restrictive encounters improves the occasion's perceivability as well as gives an open door to forces to be reckoned with to make content in a special setting.

**Identifiable Measurements:** Using identifiable measurements, for example, commitment rates, reach, and change, permits retail outlets to quantify the effect of powerhouse joint efforts. Breaking down these measurements helps in surveying the outcome of missions and refining future techniques.

### Computerized Promoting Instruments and Advances

The joining of innovation into computerized advertising endeavors improves the general viability of advancing retail plazas. Utilizing progressed devices and advancements takes into consideration designated crusades, customized encounters, and continuous investigation.

**Information Examination:** Using information investigation devices empowers malls to accumulate experiences into customer conduct, inclinations, and patterns. This information driven approach illuminates independent direction, taking into consideration the improvement of showcasing techniques in view of substantial proof.

**Personalization:** Customizing the shopping experience through designated advertising efforts, customized offers, and custom-made content further develops commitment. Computerized advertising instruments empower the division of the crowd and the conveyance of content that resounds with explicit socioeconomics.

**Expanded Reality (AR) and Augmented Reality (VR):** Incorporating AR and VR advancements into computerized promoting endeavors gives vivid encounters to customers. Virtual attempt ons, intuitive guides, and virtual walkthroughs upgrade commitment and make paramount communications.

**Area Based Showcasing:** Utilizing area based advertising instruments permits retail outlets to send designated messages, advancements, and alarms to customers in view of their closeness. This constant correspondence empowers quick activity.

**Versatile Applications:** Fostering a devoted portable application for the retail outlet improves the computerized insight for customers. Highlights, for example, in-application advancements, devotion projects, and versatile installments add to a consistent and helpful shopping venture.

**Chatbots and simulated intelligence driven Client care:** Carrying out chatbots controlled by man-made brainpower (man-made intelligence) upgrades client support by giving moment reactions to requests. Man-made intelligence driven arrangements can examine customer conduct and inclinations, presenting customized suggestions.

### Internet business Reconciliation and Omnichannel Experience

As the lines among physical and advanced retail keep on obscuring, the mix of web based business capacities and the making of an omnichannel experience become urgent parts of computerized showcasing for malls.

**Internet Shopping Stages:** Giving a web-based stage where customers can investigate items, actually look at accessibility, and make buys broadens the retail outlet's arrive at past its actual limits. Web based business coordination takes into consideration consistent exchanges and takes care of the inclinations of advanced first customers.

**Snap and-Gather Administrations:** Offering snap and-gather administrations permits customers to make online buys and get their orders at the retail outlet. This overcomes any issues among on the web and disconnected encounters, giving accommodation to customers.

**Advanced Dependability Projects:** Carrying out computerized devotion programs through portable applications or online stages empowers rehash visits and cultivates client faithfulness. Compensating customers for both on the web and in-store buys makes a strong omnichannel experience.

**Brought together Marking Across Channels:** Keeping a steady brand personality across both physical and computerized channels is fundamental for making a bound together encounter. Visual consistency, informing cognizance, and a consistent change among on the web and disconnected collaborations add to major areas of strength for a conspicuous brand.

### Estimating Adequacy and Variation Systems

Estimating the viability of computerized showcasing procedures is fundamental for upgrading efforts and guaranteeing a profit from speculation. Key execution markers (KPIs) and examination give important experiences into the effect of different drives.

**Commitment Measurements:** Following commitment measurements, like preferences, offers, remarks, and navigate rates, checks the degree of crowd communication with the retail plaza's computerized content. High commitment shows reverberation with the interest group.

**Transformation Rates:** Examining change rates, whether it be online buys, occasion participation, or recruits for devotion programs, gauges the adequacy of advanced promoting in driving wanted activities from the crowd.

**Pedestrian activity Examination:** Using innovation, like signals or geofencing, to investigate people walking through designs inside the retail outlet gives bits of knowledge into the effect of advanced advertising on actual visits. This information helps in refining systems to drive more on location commitment.

**Profit from Speculation (return for money invested):** Working out the return for capital invested of computerized advertising drives includes surveying the expenses caused versus the advantages acquired. This exhaustive assessment illuminates choices about asset portion and the prioritization of powerful channels.

**Customer Input and Reviews:** Direct criticism from customers, gathered through studies or criticism structures, offers subjective bits of knowledge into their encounters. Grasping customer fulfillment, inclinations, and problem areas guides variation techniques.

**A/B Testing:** Leading A/B testing on different computerized showcasing components, for example, promotion creatives, informing, or advancement designs, considers information driven independent direction. Distinguishing what reverberates most with the crowd refines future missions.

Variation procedures are fundamental for remaining dexterous in the unique computerized scene. Routinely surveying the viability of advanced promoting drives and being willing to emphasize in light of information driven experiences guarantees that the retail plaza stays pertinent and full with its crowd.

# Chapter 8

### Challenges and Future Trends

The scene of difficulties and future patterns traverses a huge range of spaces, addressing innovation, society, the climate, and then some. Exploring this mind boggling territory requires a nuanced comprehension of the interconnected powers forming our reality. In this investigation, we dig into the diverse difficulties defying us today and companion into the fogs representing things to come, looking to perceive the arising patterns that will shape the direction of our aggregate process.

At the front line of contemporary difficulties is the quick speed of mechanical headway. While innovation has without a doubt upset different parts of our lives, it has likewise induced a large group of phenomenal difficulties. One such test is the moral pickles emerging from the organization of man-made reasoning (artificial intelligence) and AI (ML) frameworks. As these advances become progressively coordinated into our regular routines, inquiries concerning security, responsibility, and predisposition pose a potential threat.

The inescapable impact of web-based entertainment is one more aspect of the innovative test. The democratization of data has achieved a time of phenomenal availability, however it has likewise brought about issues like falsehood, cyberbullying, and the disintegration of protection. The cultural ramifications of innovation are significant, requesting a sensitive harmony among development and the protection of human qualities.

Pair with mechanical difficulties, ecological worries cast a long shadow over what's in store. The ghost of environmental change, driven by human exercises, represents an existential danger to the planet. Increasing temperatures, outrageous climate occasions, and the consumption of regular assets request earnest and composed worldwide activity. The sensitive harmony of biological systems is under attack, and the repercussions of ecological debasement resound across friendly, monetary, and international circles.

On the cultural front, imbalances persevere as an obstinate test. The computerized partition, monetary inconsistencies, and fundamental disparities keep on sabotaging the texture of social orders around the world. Connecting these holes requires redistributive strategies as well as an essential reexamination of cultural designs. The mission for civil rights converges with issues of race, orientation, and admittance to schooling and medical care, requesting an all encompassing and comprehensive methodology.

The international scene is overflowing with difficulties that rise above public boundaries. The ascent of populism, the disintegration of global establishments, and the apparition of contention pose a potential threat. Issues like atomic multiplication, psychological warfare, and the uprooting of populaces because of contention and abuse highlight the requirement for purposeful worldwide endeavors to encourage harmony, security, and collaboration.

Financial difficulties, as well, shape the forms of our aggregate future. The digitalization of economies, computerization, and the gig economy present the two open doors and traps. The dislodging of customary positions, the requirement for upskilling, and the moral contemplations of a quickly developing financial scene request proactive and versatile techniques.

In the midst of these difficulties, a string of mechanical hopefulness winds through the texture representing things to come. Developments in sustainable power, biotechnology, and space investigation offer hints of something to look forward to. The tackling of clean energy sources, the potential for leap forwards in clinical science, and the investigation of new outskirts in space present roads for tending to the absolute most squeezing difficulties confronting mankind.

What's to come drifts that will shape our direction are profoundly interwoven with the current difficulties. The advancement of man-made reasoning and AI is ready to reclassify the idea of work, with the potential for both work creation and uprooting. The moral contemplations encompassing artificial intelligence and ML will progressively come to the front, requiring powerful structures and guidelines to guarantee capable turn of events and arrangement.

Biotechnology holds the commitment of groundbreaking headways in medical services, horticulture, and ecological protection. CRISPR quality altering innovation, specifically, opens up additional opportunities for treating hereditary sicknesses and improving the versatility of yields. Nonetheless, the moral ramifications of dabbling with the structure blocks of life bring up significant issues that request cautious thought.

The coming of 5G innovation proclaims another period of network, empowering quicker and more solid correspondence. This has suggestions for a great many ventures, from medical care and instruction to shrewd urban communities and independent vehicles. In any case, the rollout of 5G likewise achieves concerns security, network safety, and potential wellbeing chances, highlighting the requirement for hearty administrative structures.

Space investigation is encountering a renaissance, with both public and confidential substances wandering into the universe. The potential for lunar and Martian colonization, combined with progressions in space the travel industry, coaxes humankind to extend its compass past Earth. Notwithstanding, the moral contemplations of room investigation, including issues of heavenly asset abuse and the protection of extraterrestrial conditions, merit cautious assessment.

As we look into the future, the intermingling of innovations is a characterizing pattern. The incorporation of man-made intelligence, biotechnology, and nanotechnology holds the potential for extraordinary forward leaps. The improvement of supposed "meeting innovations" has the ability to reshape enterprises, upgrade human capacities, and address probably the most obstinate difficulties confronting mankind.

The nexus of supportability and innovation is another remarkable pattern. The basic to address environmental change is driving developments in environmentally friendly power, economical farming, and round economies. The quest for an additional manageable and fair future is progressively turning into a main impetus for mechanical development, with the acknowledgment that arrangements should be both viable and earth cognizant.

In the domain of medical care, the union of information examination, genomics, and customized medication is ready to reform the determination and therapy of sicknesses. The capacity to tackle huge measures of wellbeing information, combined with progresses in how we might interpret hereditary qualities, holds the commitment of additional exact and designated clinical mediations. Notwithstanding, the moral ramifications of information security, hereditary testing, and the potential for segregation in light of hereditary data bring up complex moral issues.

Training is going through a change filled by computerized innovations. The ascent of internet learning, virtual homerooms, and intelligent instructive stages is reshaping conventional models of schooling. The democratization of information, worked with by advanced devices, can possibly span instructive holes and engage students around the world. Nonetheless, difficulties, for example, the computerized partition and the requirement for a reconsidered teaching method should be addressed to open the maximum capacity of computerized instruction.

The eventual fate of work is a dynamic and developing scene. Computerization and man-made consciousness are reshaping enterprises and occupation markets, requesting a change in outlook by they way we approach schooling and labor force improvement.

The ascent of remote work, the gig economy, and adaptable work courses of action are modifying conventional thoughts of business. Finding some kind of harmony between innovative proficiency and the human component of work is really difficult for what's in store.

The convergence of morals and innovation will be a persevering through subject in the unfurling story representing things to come. As innovation turns out to be progressively enmeshed in each feature of our lives, inquiries of protection, responsibility, and the moral utilization of information become central. The improvement of moral systems, legitimate guidelines, and a culture of capable development are basic to guaranteeing that innovation serves humankind instead of enslaving it to unseen side-effects.

The job of states in exploring the difficulties and chances representing things to come is critical. Policymakers should wrestle with the ramifications of arising advancements, plan administrative structures that encourage development while defending public interests, and explore the complex international scene. Worldwide coordinated effort and tact will be fundamental in tending to worldwide difficulties that rise above public boundaries.

Environmental change moderation and transformation address a dire and existential objective. The future will observer a developing accentuation on supportable practices, environmentally friendly power sources, and roundabout economies. The progress to a low-carbon future requests mechanical development as well as purposeful worldwide endeavors to reorient monetary frameworks and utilization designs.

In the social circle, the advanced unrest is reshaping the way that we make, consume, and share data and workmanship. The democratization of content creation, worked with by computerized stages, has led to new types of articulation and correspondence. Be that as it may, this democratization is joined by difficulties, for example, the spread of disinformation, the disintegration of customary media models, and the requirement for new structures to safeguard protected innovation in the computerized age.

The fate of transportation is going through a seismic shift. The ascent of electric vehicles, independent driving innovation, and inventive transportation models messenger a more reasonable and effective time of versatility. Be that as it may, difficulties like the improvement of foundation, administrative structures, and the moral contemplations of simulated intelligence driven transportation frameworks should be addressed to open the maximum capacity of these headways.

In the domain of network protection, the future will be set apart by a heightening weapons contest between digital dangers and guard components. As our dependence on advanced innovations extends, the security of basic framework, delicate information, and individual protection becomes principal.

The improvement of vigorous network protection conventions, worldwide collaboration, and a proactive way to deal with recognizing and relieving digital dangers will be basic in defending the computerized domain.

The elements of worldwide wellbeing will keep on forming the future, with the continuous difficulties presented by irresistible sicknesses, pandemics, and the basic of general medical care. The examples gained from the Coronavirus pandemic highlight the requirement for an organized worldwide reaction, interest in general wellbeing framework, and the improvement of versatile medical services frameworks fit for adjusting to unanticipated difficulties.

As we explore the difficulties and patterns representing things to come, the significance of schooling and data proficiency couldn't possibly be more significant. Engaging people to basically survey data, explore computerized scenes, and adjust to developing innovations is fundamental in cultivating a versatile and informed worldwide populace. The development of a learning outlook and the capacity to adjust to change will be irreplaceable characteristics despite a consistently developing future.

### 8.1 Common challenges faced by shopping centers

Malls, when clamoring centers of trade and social cooperation, are wrestling with a horde of difficulties that are reshaping their part in the retail scene. The seismic changes in customer conduct, mechanical progressions, and developing cultural assumptions have combined to establish a perplexing and dynamic climate. Among the normal difficulties looked by malls, the computerized unrest poses a potential threat as a groundbreaking power.

The ascent of web based business has generally modified the manner in which purchasers shop, representing a huge test to conventional physical retail. The accommodation of web based shopping, combined with the capacity to peruse and buy from the solace of one's home, has prompted a decrease in people walking through to actual stores. Malls are confronted with the overwhelming assignment of rethinking their offer in a period where the limit between the advanced and actual domains is progressively permeable.

Additionally, the Coronavirus pandemic has sped up the reception of web based shopping, as lockdowns and social removing estimates provoked buyers to go to online business for their retail needs. Retail outlets, previously battling with the effect of web based business, ended up wrestling with the existential danger presented by the pandemic. The basic for wellbeing and security further drove customers from swarmed shopping centers, intensifying the difficulties looked by customary retail spaces.

The changing socioeconomics and inclinations of purchasers add one more layer of intricacy to the difficulties defying retail outlets. Twenty to thirty year olds and Age Z, portrayed by their computerized nativity, focus on encounters over material belongings.

This change in customer outlook has moved the interest for vivid and special retail encounters, provoking malls to advance past simple conditional spaces.

The idea of "retailtainment," mixing retail and diversion, has arisen as a reaction to this interest for experiential shopping. Malls are presently entrusted with arranging drawing in and intelligent encounters that go past the conditional part of retail. Consolidating components like spring up stores, live exhibitions, and intelligent establishments becomes critical in drawing in and holding the consideration of the advanced shopper.

The inescapability of innovation presents the two amazing open doors and difficulties for retail plazas. While computerized devices offer roads for improving the shopping experience, they additionally raise worries about information protection and security. The incorporation of innovations like expanded reality (AR) and computer generated reality (VR) holds the possibility to establish vivid and customized shopping conditions. Notwithstanding, the mindful utilization of client information and defending against digital dangers are vital contemplations in the execution of these advances.

The advancement of purchaser assumptions stretches out to the domain of maintainability. Current customers are progressively aware of natural and moral contemplations, impacting their buying choices. Malls are constrained to embrace maintainable practices, from energy-productive framework to eco-accommodating retail rehearses. The interest for morally obtained items and eco-cognizant brands requires retail plazas to reexamine their inhabitant blend and line up with the upsides of socially cognizant purchasers.

The spatial elements of retail outlets face difficulties in the time of adaptable and remote work plans. The customary model of anchor occupants and long haul leases is being reconsidered as retailers rethink their space necessities. The shift towards online deals has provoked a few retailers to focus on circulation communities over far reaching retail spaces, prompting a reconfiguration of the occupant blend inside malls.

Stopping, when a pervasive element of retail plazas, faces difficulties with regards to urbanization, maintainability objectives, and changing transportation designs. The rising accentuation on open transportation, cycling, and ride-sharing administrations challenges the traditional dependence on enormous parking garages. Retail outlets are constrained to reconsider their way to deal with stopping, consolidating multimodular transportation choices and feasible plan standards.

The cutthroat scene for malls stretches out past the limits of customary retail. The appearance of blended use improvements, enveloping private, business, and sporting components, represents an impressive test. Purchasers, particularly in metropolitan conditions, look for coordinated spaces that offer a consistent mix of living, working, and relaxation. Malls should advance into energetic local area center points that rise above the regular limits of retail.

Monetary contemplations further compound the difficulties looked by retail plazas. Monetary slumps, as exemplified by the worldwide monetary emergency of 2008 and the financial repercussions of the Coronavirus pandemic, influence buyer spending designs and renting elements. The instability of the monetary scene requires nimbleness and vital anticipating the piece of retail plaza administrators to climate financial vulnerabilities and adjust to changing economic situations.

The obscuring of lines among physical and advanced retail spaces leads to the peculiarity of omnichannel retailing. Customers presently expect a consistent mix of on the web and disconnected shopping encounters, with the capacity to peruse, buy, and return across various channels. Retail plazas should put resources into vigorous advanced framework, including web based business stages and versatile applications, to take care of the inclinations of the omnichannel purchaser.

The test of significance despite developing customer conduct is additionally exacerbated by the ascent of direct-to-buyer (DTC) brands. These carefully local brands influence online stages to lay out an immediate association with purchasers, bypassing conventional retail channels. Malls should wrestle with the need to draw in and hold these arising DTC brands, encouraging a cooperative relationship that improves the general allure of the retail space.

The repeating idea of style and purchaser patterns represents a continuous test for retail outlets. Remaining in front of quickly evolving inclinations, styles, and arising brands requires a proactive way to deal with occupant curation and key organizations. The capacity to expect and adjust to moving customer tastes is a pivotal determinant of a retail plaza's supported pertinence in a cutthroat market.

In the mission for separation, retail plazas are progressively investigating imaginative renting models. Ideas like spring up stores, turning inhabitants, and adaptable momentary leases give roads to trial and error and variety inside the retail space. These models offer a dynamic and consistently changing shopping climate, taking care of the craving for curiosity and disclosure among current buyers.

The social element of retail outlets faces difficulties in cultivating a feeling of local area and inclusivity. As actual get-together spaces, retail outlets assume a part in forming the social texture of networks. The need to establish conditions that are inviting to different socioeconomics, comprehensive of different social and gatherings, and open to people with assorted capacities is foremost. Retail outlets should advance past value-based spaces to become comprehensive local area centers that mirror the variety of their environmental elements.

Administrative contemplations additionally shape the working climate for retail outlets. Drafting regulations, building regulations, and ecological guidelines impact the turn of events and extension of retail spaces. Exploring the administrative scene requires coordinated effort with neighborhood specialists, adherence to maintainability guidelines, and a proactive way to deal with consistence.

The speed increase of mechanical reception in light of the pandemic has suggestions for the labor force inside retail outlets. Robotization, man-made consciousness, and information investigation are changing functional cycles, from stock administration to client care. Retail outlet administrators should explore the sensitive harmony between utilizing innovative efficiencies and protecting the human touch that upgrades the client experience.

All in all, retail outlets wind up at a junction, exploring a scene characterized by computerized disturbance, changing customer assumptions, and dynamic market influences. The difficulties they face are diverse, requiring a comprehensive and versatile way to deal with stay pertinent and strong. Embracing development, manageability, and a client driven ethos will be critical in forming the eventual fate of malls as they advance into dynamic and comprehensive spaces that rise above the conventional limits of retail. The capacity to explore these difficulties will decide the job malls play in the continuous story of the retail business and local area life.

## 8.2 Trends shaping the future of shopping centers, including experiential retail

The eventual fate of retail plazas is going through a significant change, formed by a conjunction of patterns that mirror the developing necessities and inclinations of purchasers. In the midst of the difficulties presented by online business, evolving socioeconomics, and cultural movements, malls are embracing imaginative procedures to reclassify their part in the retail scene. One unmistakable pattern forming the fate of malls is the change in outlook towards experiential retail.

Experiential retail addresses a takeoff from the conventional value-based model, where buyers visit malls exclusively to make buys. All things being equal, experiential retail tries to establish vivid and drawing in conditions that go past the demonstration of trading. The accentuation is on cultivating critical and genuinely resounding encounters that take special care of the advanced customer's craving for amusement, personalization, and social association.

One feature of experiential retail is the mix of innovation to upgrade the shopping experience. Increased reality (AR) and augmented reality (VR) advances are being utilized to establish intelligent and vivid conditions inside retail plazas. Buyers can utilize AR applications to imagine how furniture would search in their homes or take a stab at virtual outfits utilizing VR, obscuring the lines between the computerized and actual domains.

Besides, the ascent of intuitive showcases, brilliant mirrors, and computerized signage adds to a more powerful and drawing in shopping climate. These innovations give data and suggestions as well as make a feeling of intuitiveness that resounds with educated shoppers. The combination of computerized components upgrades the general mood of malls, making the actual space really engaging and important in an undeniably advanced world.

Experiential retail additionally appears as arranged occasions and actuations inside malls. Spring up stores, live exhibitions, and intelligent establishments add to an energetic and steadily evolving scene. These occasions make a feeling of oddity and fervor, empowering rehash visits and cultivating a local area of connected and faithful clients. Malls are developing into social centers where purchasers could shop at any point as well as take part in social and sporting encounters.

Because of the interest for experiential retail, malls are enhancing their inhabitant blend. Past customary retailers, there is a developing accentuation on consolidating diversion, eating, and wellbeing contributions. The mix of films, wellness focuses, and connoisseur feasting foundations changes retail outlets into far reaching way of life objections. This enhancement takes special care of the comprehensive necessities of buyers, situating retail plazas as spots to make buys as well as to mingle, unwind, and enjoy relaxation exercises.

The idea of "retailtainment" is fundamental to the experiential retail pattern. This combination of retail and diversion tries to make a consistent mix of shopping and relaxation. From intelligent showcases and vivid presentations to live exhibitions and themed occasions, malls are becoming stages for an assortment of diversion encounters. The objective is to enamor the customer's consideration and proposition a getaway from the everyday practice, changing shopping into a charming and critical trip.

Buyer inclinations, especially among more youthful socioeconomics, are directing the experiential retail pattern. Recent college grads and Age Z, who focus on encounters over material belongings, are driving the interest for connecting with and Instagram-commendable minutes. Retail outlets, perceiving this shift, are putting resources into establishing tastefully satisfying conditions that act as backgrounds for online entertainment sharing. The capacity to arrange outwardly engaging spaces upgrades the allure of malls as objections for mingling and self-articulation.

The mix of manageability into the experiential retail model is another imperative pattern. Shoppers, particularly more youthful ages, are progressively aware of ecological and moral contemplations. Retail outlets are answering by taking on eco-accommodating works on, advancing manageable brands, and integrating green spaces into their plan. The accentuation on manageability lines up with the upsides of socially cognizant buyers, adding to a positive brand picture and encouraging a feeling of obligation towards the climate.

Joint efforts and organizations assume a significant part in improving the experiential retail presenting inside malls. Teaming up with neighborhood specialists, planners, and social powerhouses adds an interesting and valid touch to the shopping experience. Restricted release coordinated efforts and select item dispatches make a need to keep moving and restrictiveness, tempting customers to visit retail outlets to be important for these exceptional minutes.

The mix of portable innovation is a key empowering influence of experiential retail. Portable applications and computerized stages give an extension between the physical and advanced domains, proposing customized suggestions, selective advancements, and consistent exchanges. Retail outlets are utilizing versatile innovation to upgrade the general client venture, from pre-visit wanting to in-store route and post-buy commitment. Portable applications likewise work with dependability programs, empowering rehash visits and encouraging a feeling of association with customers.

In the time of experiential retail, the actual plan and format of malls are developing to focus on open, adaptable, and welcoming spaces. The customary encased shopping center model is giving method for opening air and blended use improvements that accentuate walkability, vegetation, and local area spaces. The objective is to establish a climate that supports investigation and social connection, creating some distance from the inflexible formats of the past.

Information examination and man-made brainpower (computer based intelligence) are instrumental in customizing the experiential retail venture. By bridling information on shopper inclinations, shopping conduct, and segment patterns, malls can fit their contributions and encounters to meet the particular necessities of their ideal interest group. Man-made intelligence fueled chatbots and menial helpers further upgrade the client experience by giving ongoing help and suggestions.

The combination of on the web and disconnected retail, frequently alluded to as omnichannel retailing, is an essential piece of the experiential retail pattern. Retail outlets are utilizing computerized channels to expand the client venture past the actual store. Highlights like snap and-gather administrations, virtual customer facing facades, and expanded reality take a stab at encounters make a consistent progress among on the web and disconnected shopping. This omnichannel approach permits retail plazas to meet customers where they are, whether in the actual space or the computerized domain.

Local area commitment and social obligation are becoming focal fundamentals of experiential retail. Malls are perceiving their job as local area center points and are effectively captivating with neighborhood occupants and associations. Facilitating people group occasions, supporting nearby causes, and teaming up with neighborhood drives add to a feeling of social union and position malls as fundamental pieces of the networks they serve.

The advancement of installment techniques is likewise affecting the experiential retail scene. Contactless installments, portable wallets, and other inventive installment arrangements upgrade the proficiency and accommodation of exchanges. Credit only exchanges line up with the consistent and educated experience that experiential retail plans to give, diminishing contact in the buying system and smoothing out the general client venture.

The Coronavirus pandemic has acquainted new contemplations with the experiential retail pattern. Wellbeing and security measures, including social separating and improved cleanliness rehearses, have become vital. Malls are adjusting by carrying out touchless innovations, improving cleaning conventions, and reconfiguring spaces to oblige safe removing. The pandemic has sped up the reception of computerized devices, like virtual lines and contactless installments, further molding the development of experiential retail in a post-pandemic world.

All in all, experiential retail is an extraordinary pattern that is reshaping the fate of malls. As purchasers look for something other than items during their shopping processes, the accentuation on making vivid, engaging, and socially captivating encounters has turned into an essential objective. Malls that effectively coordinate experiential components into their contributions are ready to get by as well as flourish in a retail scene characterized by computerized disturbance and changing purchaser assumptions. The capacity to adjust, advance, and make convincing encounters will be vital in deciding the outcome of malls in the dynamic and cutthroat retail climate representing things to come.

## 8.3 Strategies for staying competitive in a changing retail landscape

The retail scene is going through a significant change, pushed by moving shopper ways of behaving, mechanical headways, and dynamic market influences. Remaining serious in this consistently advancing climate expects retailers to embrace imaginative methodologies that address current difficulties as well as position them for supported progress from here on out. From embracing internet business and omnichannel retailing to focusing on client experience and utilizing information examination, retailers are exploring a complicated territory to stay important and serious.

One critical methodology for remaining cutthroat is the consistent reconciliation of internet business into the general retail technique. The ascent of internet shopping has reclassified customer assumptions, and retailers should adjust to this computerized shift. Laying out a hearty and easy to use internet business stage empowers retailers to contact a more extensive crowd, take special care of the inclinations of educated customers, and give helpful admittance to items and administrations.

Omnichannel retailing addresses an all encompassing methodology that recognizes the interconnectedness of on the web and disconnected channels. Retailers are perceiving the significance of making a brought together and steady insight across different touchpoints.

Whether a client is perusing items internet, visiting an actual store, or connecting through online entertainment, the omnichannel system guarantees a consistent and coordinated venture. Highlights like snap and-gather, in-store get, and synchronized stock frameworks overcome any issues among on the web and disconnected, giving shoppers adaptability and accommodation.

Chasing after seriousness, the attention on client experience has become central. Past the value-based nature of retail, making a positive and important client experience cultivates steadfastness and rehash business. Retailers are putting resources into customized administrations, mindful client care, and taking part in store encounters to separate themselves in a jam-packed market. The capacity to interface with clients on a profound level and expect their requirements adds to a positive brand insight.

The job of information examination in remaining cutthroat couldn't possibly be more significant. Retailers are utilizing huge information and man-made reasoning to acquire experiences into purchaser conduct, inclinations, and patterns. Breaking down information permits retailers to settle on informed choices in regards to stock administration, valuing methodologies, and customized showcasing efforts. Prescient examination expects shifts in buyer interest, empowering retailers to remain in front of patterns and change their contributions as needs be.

Personalization has arisen as a critical methodology for retailers trying to improve client commitment. By utilizing client information, retailers can tailor their contributions, suggestions, and advertising messages to individual inclinations. Customized shopping encounters, whether through designated advancements, item proposals, or modified content, make a feeling of eliteness and importance for the purchaser. The capacity to cause clients to feel seen and comprehended adds to mark devotion and client maintenance.

The approach of versatile innovation has reshaped the retail scene, and retailers are taking advantage of the capability of portable applications to upgrade the client experience. Versatile applications give an immediate channel to correspondence, permitting retailers to send customized offers, updates, and advancements to buyers' cell phones. Furthermore, portable applications work with consistent exchanges, reliability programs, and in-application elements, for example, expanded reality for virtual attempt ons, improving the general shopping experience.

Chasing intensity, retailers are progressively investigating the combination of expanded reality (AR) and computer generated reality (VR) advancements. AR empowers buyers to envision items in their true climate prior to making a buy, tending to worries about fit and feel. VR, then again, offers vivid and intuitive encounters, for example, virtual store visits or item shows. These advances connect with purchasers as well as separate the retail insight, making it more creative and engaging.

Supportability has turned into a characterizing factor in customer inclinations, and retailers are consolidating eco-accommodating practices into their procedures. From obtaining items from feasible providers to taking on ecologically cognizant bundling, retailers are lining up with the upsides of socially capable buyers. Imparting a guarantee to manageability upgrades brand notoriety as well as draws in a developing segment of ecologically cognizant customers.

In the journey for seriousness, retailers are investigating key coordinated efforts and associations. Coordinated efforts with different brands, powerhouses, or nearby organizations can bring a new point of view, extend the client base, and make novel contributions. Key organizations additionally give amazing open doors to co-marked drives, restrictive item dispatches, and joint showcasing endeavors, enhancing the brand's scope and pertinence.

The idea of restricted version deliveries and elite assortments has built up forward movement as a procedure to drive interest and make a need to get going. Retailers are utilizing shortage and selectiveness to create whiz around specific items, provoking shoppers to rapidly act. Whether through coordinated effort with creators, superstar supports, or occasional deliveries, restricted version methodologies tap into the mental parts of buyer conduct, driving both energy and deals.

In light of changing buyer inclinations, retailers are reexamining their actual spaces to establish seriously captivating and experiential conditions. The customary store design is developing into a dynamic and intelligent space where purchasers can investigate, collaborate, and find items. Retailers are putting resources into store plan, visual marketing, and in-store occasions to make a tactile rich encounter that goes past the simple demonstration of making a buy.

Web-based entertainment has arisen as an integral asset for retailers to interface with customers, fabricate brand mindfulness, and drive commitment. Retailers are utilizing stages like Instagram, Facebook, and TikTok to exhibit items, share in the background content, and communicate with their crowd. Virtual entertainment powerhouses and client created content add to the virality of items, making a buzz that broadens the range of the brand.

In the domain of cutthroat procedures, quick and adaptable production network the executives is vital. The capacity to adjust to changes popular, answer rapidly to showcase drifts, and streamline stock levels is an upper hand. Retailers are investigating advancements, for example, blockchain for improved straightforwardness in the store network, prescient examination for request determining, and lithe strategies answers for smooth out the development of merchandise.

Membership based models are acquiring noticeable quality as a system for encouraging client steadfastness and guaranteeing a consistent income stream. Retailers are offering membership benefits that give buyers arranged items, restrictive access, or customary conveyances.

These models make a feeling of comfort for the buyer while laying out a repetitive relationship that goes past individual exchanges.

Computerized reasoning (computer based intelligence) is progressively being sent in retail to upgrade functional productivity and client experience. Simulated intelligence controlled chatbots give moment client service, menial helpers propose customized suggestions, and AI calculations dissect tremendous measures of information for significant experiences. Mechanizing routine errands permits retailers to zero in on essential navigation and development, adding to generally speaking seriousness.

Chasing serious separation, retailers are reconsidering the job of actual stores. Past being value-based spaces, stores are becoming centers for brand encounters, local area commitment, and experiential retail. Retailers are trying different things with intelligent presentations, in-store occasions, and vivid innovations to make an objective where shoppers need to invest energy, encouraging a feeling of association with the brand.

Dynamic valuing methodologies are assuming a significant part in remaining serious, especially in the period of web based business. Retailers are utilizing calculations and constant information to change evaluating in view of variables, for example, request, contender valuing, and stock levels. Dynamic evaluating improves income as well as permits retailers to answer quickly to advertise elements and customer conduct.

In the period of globalization, retailers are investigating worldwide development as a technique for development and seriousness. Entering new business sectors gives admittance to different buyer socioeconomics, grows the client base, and mitigates chances related with reliance on a solitary market. In any case, effective global extension requires cautious thought of social subtleties, administrative scenes, and nearby market elements.

The development of voice trade, driven by menial helpers like Amazon's Alexa and Google Colleague, is reshaping the retail scene. Retailers are enhancing their internet based presence for voice search, making voice-initiated shopping encounters, and investigating organizations with remote helper stages. Voice trade addresses another outskirts in purchaser cooperations, and retailers taking on early can acquire an upper hand.

The retail scene is going through a significant and quick change, formed by a combination of mechanical progressions, moving shopper ways of behaving, and worldwide financial changes. This unique development isn't only a repetitive shift yet a crucial rebuilding of how organizations work and how purchasers draw in with the market. As we explore this changing retail scene, a few critical patterns and powers come to the very front, enlightening the difficulties and open doors that retailers face chasing importance and achievement.

**Internet business Unrest**

At the core of the changing retail scene is the certain impact of web based business. The ascent of internet shopping stages has upset customary physical retail models, convincing retailers to recalibrate their procedures to oblige the inclinations of a carefully engaged shopper base. The comfort, openness, and immense item choice presented by web based business stages have moved the overall influence, making on the web directs a predominant power in the retail environment.

Customary retailers are not only rivaling one another; they are fighting with behemoths like Amazon that have reclassified client assumptions. This requires an essential coordination of online business into the general retail approach, recognizing the significance of computerized channels as essential roads for client commitment and exchanges. Whether through committed web-based customer facing facades, commercial center associations, or omnichannel methodologies, retailers should embrace the computerized domain to stay serious in this developing scene.

**Omnichannel Retailing**

The development of omnichannel retailing addresses an essential reaction to the obscuring lines among on the web and disconnected shopping encounters. Buyers presently anticipate a consistent change between different channels, from perusing items online to making buys coming up or the other way around. The omnichannel approach brings together these unique touchpoints, giving a steady and coordinated client venture.

Retailers are embracing advances that work with omnichannel methodologies, like stock synchronization, snap and-gather benefits, and brought together client profiles. The objective is to make an all encompassing shopping experience that rises above individual channels, perceiving that clients frequently move smoothly among on the web and disconnected collaborations. The outcome of an omnichannel procedure depends on the capacity to convey a durable and interconnected brand insight across all buyer touchpoints.

### Experiential Retail

As the retail scene develops, the idea of experiential retail has arisen as a key differentiator. Past simple exchanges, purchasers look for vivid and drawing in encounters while associating with brands. Experiential retail goes past the practical parts of shopping; it expects to make close to home associations and enduring recollections for buyers.

Retailers are rethinking actual spaces to focus on experiential components, consolidating intuitive presentations, virtual attempt ons, and in-store occasions. The objective is to change the demonstration of shopping into a multisensory venture, captivating purchasers to invest more energy coming up and encouraging a more profound association with the brand. The accentuation on experiential retail is a reaction to the changing assumptions for buyers, especially more youthful socioeconomics who focus on encounters over belongings.

### Information Driven Retail

In the period of data, information has turned into an incredible asset for retailers trying to grasp customer conduct, customize encounters, and streamline tasks. Information driven retail includes the assortment, examination, and use of huge measures of information to illuminate key navigation. Retailers saddle client information to acquire bits of knowledge into inclinations, shopping examples, and patterns, considering more designated promoting endeavors and customized proposals.

Man-made brainpower (artificial intelligence) and AI calculations assume a critical part in handling and deciphering information, empowering retailers to foresee customer conduct and streamline stock administration. From dynamic evaluating procedures to customized advertising efforts, information driven retail enables organizations to pursue informed choices progressively. In any case, with the advantages of information driven bits of knowledge come difficulties connected with security concerns and the moral utilization of client information, requiring a sensitive harmony among personalization and shopper trust.

### Personalization and Customization

Purchasers progressively look for customized and custom-made encounters, and retailers are answering by integrating personalization into different parts of their tasks. From customized item proposals in view of past buys to tweaking in-store communications, the objective is to cause shoppers to feel seen and comprehended. Innovation assumes an essential part in empowering personalization, with calculations breaking down information to convey individualized encounters.

Customization, then again, stretches out to permitting buyers to make or alter items to suit their inclinations. This pattern is especially noticeable in ventures like design, where brands offer customized clothing or adornments. The shift towards personalization and customization mirrors a craving for uniqueness and a takeoff from one-size-fits-all methodologies.

### Social Business

Virtual entertainment stages have become vital to the retail insight, obscuring the lines among mingling and shopping. Social trade includes the incorporation of shopping highlights straightforwardly into virtual entertainment stages, permitting customers to find and buy items without leaving the application. Stages like Instagram and Facebook have presented shoppable posts, empowering brands to grandstand items and smooth out the buying system inside the virtual entertainment climate.

Powerhouse showcasing, a subset of social business, use the impact of people with huge web-based entertainment followings to advance items and brands. Customers, especially more youthful socioeconomics, frequently seek powerhouses for item proposals and way of life motivation. The combination of online entertainment and business gives retailers new roads to associate with customers, fabricate brand mindfulness, and drive deals.

**Membership Models**

Membership based models have gotten momentum as a system for cultivating client steadfastness and making a consistent income stream. Retailers are offering membership benefits that give buyers arranged items, selective access, or standard conveyances. This model takes special care of the craving for comfort and a customized insight, with buyers buying into get items consistently, whether it's excellence items, clothing, or food things.

The membership model additionally lines up with the shift towards supportability, as it frequently includes the conveyance of organized items in eco-accommodating bundling. By giving an anticipated income stream and cultivating a feeling of continuous commitment, membership models add to long haul client connections and brand devotion.

**Manageability and Moral Utilization**

Progressively, buyers are focusing on manageability and moral contemplations in their buying choices. The attention to ecological effect, fair work rehearses, and moral obtaining has reshaped buyer assumptions, convincing retailers to embrace more supportable and socially capable practices. From eco-accommodating bundling to moral store network the executives, maintainability has turned into a center thought in the changing retail scene.

Retailers are integrating maintainability into their image informing, showcasing endeavors, and item contributions. The interest for straightforwardness in regards to obtaining and creation processes has prompted the ascent of eco-cognizant brands and accreditations. Embracing supportability lines up with buyer values as well as adds to a positive brand picture and positions retailers as dependable stewards in the worldwide commercial center.

**Globalization and Cross-Line Trade**

The changing retail scene is set apart by a rising accentuation on globalization, with retailers investigating worldwide development to take advantage of assorted customer socioeconomics. Online business stages work with cross-line trade, permitting retailers to arrive at shoppers in various nations without the requirement for an actual presence. Worldwide development presents valuable open doors for development yet in addition requires a nuanced comprehension of social subtleties, administrative scenes, and neighborhood market elements.

Cross-line web based business empowers purchasers to get to items from around the world, adding to a more interconnected worldwide commercial center. Retailers should explore strategic difficulties, cash contemplations, and differing buyer inclinations to take part in cross-line trade effectively. The capacity to adjust to different business sectors and take care of the inclinations of a worldwide purchaser base is an essential basic in the changing retail scene.

**Inventory network Flexibility**

The Coronavirus pandemic featured the weaknesses in worldwide stock chains, provoking retailers to reconsider and build up their production network systems. Production network flexibility has turned into a basic thought, with retailers trying to relieve gambles related with disturbances, whether brought about by pandemics, cataclysmic events, or international occasions. This includes broadening providers, upgrading stock administration, and putting resources into advancements that give perceivability and nimbleness in the production network.

Mechanical developments, for example, blockchain are being investigated to upgrade straightforwardness and detectability in the store network. Retailers are likewise taking on a more limited way to deal with obtaining and creation, diminishing reliance on incorporated supply chains. The accentuation on store network strength mirrors a proactive position in exploring vulnerabilities and guaranteeing a constant progression of items to satisfy shopper need.

**Ascent of Voice Trade**

The approach of remote helpers like Amazon's Alexa and Google Right hand has brought about voice trade, reshaping how shoppers collaborate with retailers. Voice business includes utilizing voice orders to look for items, add things to the shopping basket, and complete exchanges. This sans hands and conversational way to deal with shopping presents new open doors and difficulties for retailers.

Retailers are enhancing their web-based presence for voice search, guaranteeing that item data is effectively available through voice orders. Coordinating voice-actuated shopping encounters and utilizing associations with remote helper stages are techniques embraced to remain serious in this arising space. Voice trade addresses a shift towards additional normal and natural communications, expecting retailers to adjust to developing purchaser ways of behaving.

**Wellbeing and Security Contemplations**

The Coronavirus pandemic significantly affected purchaser ways of behaving and assumptions, especially concerning wellbeing and security. Retailers are adjusting to new standards by carrying out upgraded cleanliness measures, touchless advancements, and reconfiguring actual spaces to oblige social removing. The accentuation on wellbeing and security has become fundamental to the client experience, affecting in-store rehearses as well as molding how retailers convey their obligation to purchaser prosperity.

Retailers are utilizing advances like contactless installments, virtual lines, and versatile applications to limit actual contact and upgrade the general security of the shopping climate. The changing assumptions about wellbeing and security highlight the significance of deftness and responsiveness in tending to advancing shopper concerns.

**Difficulties and Valuable open doors**

In the midst of the heap of changes in the retail scene, difficulties and open doors exist together. Customary retailers face the test of adjusting to online business and omnichannel models to stay serious in a computerized first climate. The requirement for information driven bits of knowledge acquaints difficulties related with protection concerns and moral information use. Manageability drives require speculations and a pledge to dependable practices, while the ascent of social trade requests a nuanced comprehension of web-based entertainment elements.

On the other side, these difficulties present open doors for development and separation. Retailers can use innovation to upgrade the client experience, embrace maintainability to line up with buyer values, and use information driven bits of knowledge to settle on informed choices. The shift towards experiential retail permits retailers to make exceptional and paramount cooperations with shoppers, cultivating brand dependability.

The changing retail scene requires a mentality of nonstop transformation and an eagerness to embrace development. Retailers that proactively answer developing customer inclinations, influence mechanical progressions, and focus on maintainability won't just explore the difficulties yet in addition position themselves for long haul outcome in this powerful and cutthroat climate. As the retail scene keeps on developing, the capacity to remain on the ball and interface with the steadily changing necessities of shoppers will be the way to supported pertinence and development.

# Chapter 9

### Success Stories

Examples of overcoming adversity are frequently woven with strings of assurance, flexibility, and unflinching commitment. These accounts rise above existence, moving ages with their stories of win against affliction. In the domain of business venture, these adventures are especially charming, exhibiting the unstoppable human soul and its capacity to change dreams into the real world.

One such story starts in the clamoring roads of Silicon Valley, where a youthful visionary named Alex Thompson left on an excursion that would rethink the scene of innovation. Equipped with only an intense confidence in his thoughts and a voracious interest, Alex set off to make an organization that would push the limits of development. His process was laden with difficulties, from tying down beginning subsidizing to exploring the perplexing snare of the tech business.

Resolute, Alex emptied incalculable hours into refining his idea, a progressive piece of programming that vowed to change correspondence. The defining moment came when he protected a gathering with an investor able to face a challenge on his vision.

The pitch was perfect, a demonstration of Alex's fastidious readiness and relentless certainty. The financial backer saw the potential, and the seed subsidizing streamed into Alex's endeavor, denoting the introduction of an organization that would before long become inseparable from progress.

As the years unfurled, Alex's organization took off higher than ever, making a permanent imprint on the tech scene. The product he spearheaded turned into a foundation of current correspondence, utilized by millions all over the planet. The achievement didn't come for the time being; it was the aftereffect of vigorous exertion, vital navigation, and an enduring confidence in the force of advancement.

Across the mainland, in the core of New York City, another example of overcoming adversity was unfurling, but in an alternate industry. Sarah Rodriguez, a pioneer in the realm of style, had consistently held onto an energy for plan. Since early on, she portrayed dresses and imagined runway shows that would grandstand her manifestations to the world. In any case, the way to outcome in the cutthroat design industry was weighed down with deterrents.

Resolute by the doubters and energized by her innovative vision, Sarah sent off her own style mark. The good 'ol days were set apart by monetary limitations and the exhausting undertaking of laying out a brand in a market overwhelmed by laid out monsters. Nonetheless, Sarah's one of a kind plans and obligation to manageability put her aside. Gradually however consistently, her image earned respect, drawing in a devoted following of style devotees who resounded with her ethos.

Sarah's advancement came when a noticeable design magazine highlighted her assortment, lauding the combination of innovativeness and maintainability. The openness launch her image into the standard, prompting coordinated efforts with compelling figures in the design business. Sarah's prosperity was not only an individual victory; it was a demonstration of the groundbreaking force of tirelessness and a guarantee to one's standards.

In the domain of money, James Anderson arose as a light, reshaping the scene of venture with his capricious methodology. Brought up in an unassuming area, James' process started enthusiastically for numbers and a strong fascination with the elements of monetary business sectors. His initial vocation in a conventional venture company gave important bits of knowledge however left him longing for a more imaginative and dynamic methodology.

Still up in the air to manufacture his own way, James established his trading company with an emphasis on problematic advancements and developing business sectors. His antagonist technique caused a commotion in the moderate universe of money, yet James stayed relentless in his convictions. The defining moment came when one of his initial interests in a noteworthy tech startup yielded remarkable returns, grabbing the eye of the venture local area.

James' firm turned into a reference point of development, drawing in top ability and protecting organizations with state of the art organizations. His prosperity rocked the boat, demonstrating that embracing change and proceeding with reasonable plans of action could yield remarkable outcomes. Past the monetary benefits, James' story highlighted the significance of visionary administration in exploring the consistently advancing scene of worldwide business sectors.

While these examples of overcoming adversity unfurled in different businesses and geologies, they share ongoing ideas that wind through the texture of accomplishment. The primary string is the unflinching confidence in one's vision, a conviction that rises above questions and distrust. Alex, Sarah, and James confronted endless difficulties, yet their unflinching obligation to their beliefs impelled them forward.

Another pivotal component is flexibility despite difficulty. Achievement is only occasionally a direct excursion; it is set apart by difficulties, disappointments, and snapshots of uncertainty. What separates the victorious from the crushed is the capacity to quickly return, gain from misfortunes, and use disappointments as venturing stones toward progress. Alex's underlying battles for subsidizing, Sarah's difficulties in the serious style industry, and James' capricious venture approach all expected versatility in overflow.

Besides, essential dynamic assumed a urgent part in these examples of overcoming adversity. Every hero needed to explore a complicated scene, settling on decisions that would shape the direction of their undertakings. Whether it was Alex's pitch to get funding, Sarah's choice to focus on supportability in her plans, or James' antagonist speculation methodology, these pioneers displayed a sharp comprehension of their separate businesses and the capacity to go with determined choices.

Cooperation and systems administration likewise assumed a critical part in these stories. Achievement seldom happens in segregation; it is much of the time the consequence of significant organizations, mentorship, and a strong organization. Alex profited from the mentorship of experienced business people who directed him through the complexities of the tech business. Sarah's coordinated efforts with compelling figures in the style world extended her image's scope, while James' organizations with imaginative organizations filled the outcome of his venture company.

Development arose as a typical subject across these examples of overcoming adversity. Every hero disturbed laid out standards and spearheaded novel methodologies in their particular fields. Alex's notable programming, Sarah's combination of inventiveness and supportability, and James' emphasis on arising innovations generally mirrored a pledge to development as an impetus for progress.

The more extensive ramifications of these examples of overcoming adversity stretch out past the singular accomplishments of Alex, Sarah, and James. They act as guides of motivation for yearning business people, creatives, and visionaries, showing that fantasies can for sure be converted into reality with the right mix of assurance, strength, vital reasoning, cooperation, and advancement.

As the stories of progress keep on unfurling in different corners of the world, they paint a mosaic of human potential and the boundless conceivable outcomes that exist in the grip of those able to leave on the difficult excursion of transforming dreams into the real world. Examples of overcoming adversity are not simply stories of win; they are outlines for the people who hope against hope, offering direction and motivation to explore the exciting bends in the road of their novel processes.

In the domain of innovation, a gathering of youthful designers in a carport set off to rethink the manner in which individuals collaborate with data. Their vision was aggressive: to make a web crawler that could coordinate the huge span of the web and convey pertinent outcomes with exceptional exactness. Larry Page and Sergey Brin, the organizers behind Google, set out on an excursion that would change the computerized scene.

In the good 'ol days, Google confronted suspicion and rivalry from laid out players. The idea of a web crawler that could beat existing choices appeared to be daring.

Notwithstanding, Larry and Sergey's steady quest for greatness, combined with their obligation to client experience, set Google on a direction toward predominance.

The advancement accompanied the improvement of the PageRank calculation, a progressive way to deal with positioning pages in light of their importance and authority. This calculation pushed Google to the bleeding edge of the web index industry, making it the go-to stage for clients looking for data on the web. The effortlessness of the point of interaction, combined with the force of the calculation, made Google a commonly recognized name.

As Google's impact extended, so did its item contributions. The organization differentiated into email administrations, web based planning, and, surprisingly, wandered into the domain of working frameworks with Android. Every development was set apart by a pledge to advancement and a client driven approach. Google's example of overcoming adversity isn't just about search; it is a demonstration of the extraordinary force of innovation when directed by a reasonable vision and a devotion to further developing client encounters.

In the domain of diversion, the tale of Pixar Liveliness Studios stands apart as a demonstration of the marriage of imagination and innovation. Pixar's process started with a gathering of visionaries, including Steve Occupations, Ed Catmull, and John Lasseter, who shared an enthusiasm for narrating through liveliness. Their objective was not only to make vivified films however to rethink the fine art itself.

Pixar's initial days were set apart by monetary battles and the challenging undertaking of persuading the world that PC created movement could inspire feeling and recount convincing stories. The defining moment accompanied the arrival of "Toy Story" in 1995, the world's first completely PC enlivened highlight film. The progress of "Toy Story" not just settled Pixar as a power in liveliness yet in addition flagged a change in perspective in the business.

The resulting films, from "Tracking down Nemo" to "Up" and "Back to front," displayed Pixar's capacity to mix state of the art innovation with inspiring narrating. The studio's obligation to pushing the limits of what was conceivable in movement prompted a line of basic and business victories. The Pixar example of overcoming adversity is a demonstration of the groundbreaking force of innovativeness when combined with mechanical development, delineating that narrating can be raised higher than ever through the marriage of workmanship and innovation.

In the realm of web-based entertainment, the transient ascent of Facebook remains as a cutting edge example of overcoming adversity that reshaped the manner in which individuals interface and offer data. Mark Zuckerberg, an understudy enthusiastically for coding, sent off Facebook from his apartment fully intent on making a stage that would interface individuals worldwide. The underlying emphasis, restricted to Harvard understudies, immediately extended to different colleges and at last to the overall population.

Facebook's prosperity depended on its capacity to take advantage of the essential human longing for association. The stage gave a space to clients to share their lives, interface with loved ones, and draw in with a more extensive local area. As the client base developed, so did Facebook's impact, turning into a focal center for social connection on the web.

The presentation of highlights like the News source and the improvement of a powerful publicizing stage energized Facebook's monetary achievement. The organization opened up to the world in 2012 of every perhaps of the most expected first sale of stock (Initial public offerings) ever. Notwithstanding difficulties and contentions, including worries about client security and the spread of falsehood, Facebook's effect on worldwide correspondence is certain.

These examples of overcoming adversity, traversing the domains of innovation, amusement, and virtual entertainment, exhibit the different manners by which development can reshape ventures and leave a persevering through influence on society. Whether through reforming search, rethinking movement, or interfacing individuals across the globe, these accounts outline the groundbreaking force of visionary initiative, mechanical development, and a pledge to improving human encounters.

As the world keeps on advancing, new examples of overcoming adversity will without a doubt arise, driven by the tenacious quest for development and the dauntless soul of the people who hope against hope.

Whether in the domains of science, medical care, or space investigation, the following parts of examples of overcoming adversity are ready to be composed, rousing people in the future to push the limits of what is conceivable and make a heritage that rises above time.

**9.1 In-depth analysis of successful shopping centers around the world**

Effective malls all over the planet act as powerful centers that go past simple retail spaces, offering a multi-layered encounter that takes care of the different requirements and wants of shoppers. These flourishing business buildings are portrayed by essential preparation, imaginative plan, and a sharp comprehension of developing purchaser patterns. In this top to bottom examination, we will dig into the key factors that add to the outcome of noticeable malls, looking at contextual analyses from different areas.

One excellent model of an effective retail plaza is The Dubai Shopping center in the Unified Middle Easterner Emirates. Arranged at the core of Dubai's clamoring downtown locale, this monster retail and diversion complex is a demonstration of magnificence and vision. Traversing more than 12 million square feet, The Dubai Shopping center rises above the traditional idea of a shopping objective, enveloping a broad exhibit of retail outlets, feasting choices, diversion offices, and, surprisingly, an incredibly famous aquarium.

At the center of The Dubai Shopping center's prosperity is its essential area. Situated contiguous the famous Burj Khalifa, the world's tallest structure, and ignoring the hypnotizing Dubai Wellspring, the shopping center profits by the city's status as a worldwide the travel industry and business center point. The coordination of extravagance stores, lead stores, and worldwide brands takes care of a different customer base, from nearby occupants to rich sightseers looking for a top notch shopping experience.

Past its broad retail contributions, The Dubai Shopping center separates itself through its obligation to experiential amusement. The Dubai Aquarium and Submerged Zoo, situated inside the shopping center, house a great assortment of marine life, including sharks and beams. The vivid experience of strolling through a straightforward passage encompassed by oceanic marvels adds a remarkable aspect to the mall, drawing in guests looking for retail treatment as well as important encounters.

Besides, The Dubai Shopping center elements a devoted Design Road, a region that houses very good quality style brands, further hoisting its status as an extravagance shopping objective. The shopping center's fastidious consideration regarding feel and engineering loftiness adds to an outwardly enrapturing climate, improving the general shopping experience. With a sweeping scope of eating choices, including high end foundations and global foods, The Dubai Shopping center has effectively situated itself as a way of life objective that rises above the limits of customary retail spaces.

On the opposite side of the globe, Westfield London fills in as a perfect representation of a fruitful retail plaza in Europe. Situated in Shepherd's Shrub, Westfield London is one of the biggest malls in the Unified Realm, highlighting a different blend of retail, feasting, and diversion choices. Its essential situating in a flourishing metropolitan region and its obligation to mixing comfort with extravagance add to its far and wide allure.

One of the vital variables behind Westfield London's prosperity is its accentuation on making a consistent shopping experience. The mix of innovation, like advanced wayfinding frameworks and savvy stopping arrangements, improves accommodation for guests. The shopping center's format is intended to work with simple route, guaranteeing that benefactors can investigate the broad scope of stores and conveniences without feeling overpowered.

Westfield London's way to deal with occupant blend is likewise critical. By organizing a mix of high-road retailers, extravagance brands, and experiential contributions, the mall takes care of an expansive segment. The incorporation of lead stores for prestigious brands, combined with an emphasis on arising patterns and imaginative ideas, guarantees that Westfield London stays a dynamic and developing retail objective.

Besides, Westfield London puts major areas of strength for an on local area commitment and occasions. The shopping center has an assortment of social and diversion occasions over time, going from style shows to live exhibitions. This draws in neighborhood occupants as well as lays out Westfield London as a social and social center inside the local area.

In Asia, the progress of Tokyo Midtown in Japan gives experiences into the social subtleties that add to the flourishing of a retail plaza. Arranged in the upscale Roppongi region, Tokyo Midtown is a blended use improvement that consistently coordinates office spaces, extravagance homes, and retail foundations. Its multi-layered approach takes care of the requirements of metropolitan experts, inhabitants, and guests the same.

Tokyo Midtown's prosperity is attached in its capacity to mix advancement with customary Japanese style. The plan of the complex consolidates components of Japanese workmanship and culture, establishing an agreeable climate that reverberates with the neighborhood personality. The consideration of craftsmanship establishments, occasional presentations, and carefully finished gardens improves the general vibe, making Tokyo Midtown a shopping objective as well as a social and imaginative territory.

The mix of office spaces inside the perplexing adds a layer of usefulness, drawing in a constant flow of experts who add to the daytime footfall. The consistent progress from work to recreation is worked with by the presence of upscale feasting choices, extravagance stores, and social attractions. Tokyo Midtown's essential situating as a way of life objective mirrors a profound comprehension of the Japanese balance between fun and serious activities and the significance of making spaces that take care of different parts of day to day existence.

Furthermore, Tokyo Midtown's obligation to supportability lines up with the developing awareness of natural obligation among shoppers. The complex consolidates eco-accommodating practices, from energy-productive structure plans to green spaces that add to a feeling of prosperity. This lines up with the inclinations of a socially and earth cognizant buyer base, further improving the allure of Tokyo Midtown.

In North America, Shopping center of America in Minnesota stands apart as a notorious illustration of an effective retail plaza that has developed into a worldwide traveler objective. Crossing over 5.6 million square feet, Shopping center of America goes past the ordinary retail model by incorporating amusement, attractions, and cordiality. Its essential area close to Minneapolis-Holy person Paul Worldwide Air terminal and its status as the biggest shopping center in the US add to its charm.

Shopping center of America's prosperity can be credited to obligation to making an objective takes special care of a large number of interests. The shopping center houses north of 500 stores, including leader areas for significant retailers, yet it additionally includes attractions like Nickelodeon Universe, an indoor event congregation, and Ocean LIFE Minnesota, a submerged aquarium. This mix of shopping, diversion, and family-accommodating attractions positions Shopping center of America as an extensive objective for guests, everything being equal.

The shopping center's imaginative way to deal with inhabitant blend incorporates a different exhibit of retailers, from design and gadgets to specialty stores and nearby stores. The joining of experiential retail ideas, for example, intelligent display areas and themed stores, adds a component of curiosity to the shopping experience. Shopping center of America's versatility to developing purchaser drifts and its capacity to draw in both neighborhood and global guests add to its supported achievement.

Besides, Shopping center of America's obligation to local area commitment is obvious through its facilitating of occasions, going from live exhibitions and big name appearances to beneficent drives. This cultivates a feeling of having a place and positions the shopping center as a focal center point for the nearby local area. The accessibility of on location lodgings and an extensive variety of feasting choices likewise expands the guest experience, empowering longer stays and rehash visits.

These contextual investigations aggregately feature a few shared factors that add to the progress of retail plazas internationally. One of the overall subjects is the essential incorporation of different components to make an all encompassing objective. Effective malls go past being simple stores of retail outlets; they curate an encounter that envelops diversion, feasting, social commitment, and, surprisingly, private or office spaces.

Also, the flexibility of retail outlets to neighborhood and worldwide patterns is urgent. The capacity to recognize and answer shifts in shopper conduct, mechanical headways, and social inclinations guarantees that malls stay important and engaging. This versatility is exemplified by the consideration of innovation driven arrangements, the combination of supportability rehearses, and the fuse of experiential retail ideas.

The job of engineering and configuration in molding the personality of retail outlets couldn't possibly be more significant. Effective edifices give fastidious consideration to feel, establishing outwardly engaging conditions that resound with the character of the region. Whether it is the glory of The Dubai Shopping center, the consistent format of Westfield London, the combination of advancement and custom in Tokyo Midtown, or the complex attractions of Shopping center of America, compositional plan assumes a urgent part in drawing in and holding guests.

Inhabitant blend, the choice of retail marks, and the curation of contributions are basic parts of a mall's prosperity. Finding some kind of harmony between laid out extravagance brands, high-road retailers, arising fashioners, and experiential ideas guarantees that the mall requests to an expansive segment. The consideration of lead stores and select joint efforts adds a component of eliteness, drawing in knowing buyers.

Besides, the joining of innovation improves the general client experience. Advanced wayfinding frameworks, brilliant stopping arrangements, and intuitive presentations add to comfort and openness. Innovation likewise assumes a part in the domain of showcasing and client commitment, with numerous effective malls utilizing online entertainment, versatile applications, and virtual encounters to associate with their crowd.

The part of local area commitment arises as a repetitive topic in the progress of malls. Laying out a feeling of local area includes drawing in guests as well as cultivating an association with the neighborhood people. Occasions, social drives, and joint efforts with neighborhood organizations add to a feeling of spot, situating the mall as a focal center point inside the local area.

The outcome of retail outlets additionally depends on their capacity to make paramount encounters. Past the conditional idea of retail, fruitful edifices offer diversion choices, social attractions, and novel encounters that go past customary shopping. This shift toward experiential retail lines up with the changing assumptions for shoppers who look for items as well as a story, an association, and an in general enhancing experience.

## 9.2 Lessons learned from both thriving and struggling shopping centers

The retail scene is a unique field where malls, whether flourishing or battling, offer significant examples for industry partners. Inspecting both examples of overcoming adversity and difficulties looked by retail plazas gives experiences into the elements that add to supported success or expected entanglements. This extensive examination dives into the illustrations gained from different malls all over the planet, revealing insight into the methodologies that improve achievement and the entanglements that can prompt difficulties.

Flourishing retail outlets, exemplified by notorious objections like The Shopping center of America in Minnesota, give important illustrations in making a diverse encounter that goes past conventional retail. One key example is the significance of expansion, where fruitful malls coordinate diversion, attractions, and cordiality to take special care of a wide segment. Shopping center of America, as a perfect representation, joins more than 500 stores with attractions like Nickelodeon Universe and Ocean LIFE Minnesota, offering a thorough objective for guests, everything being equal.

The reconciliation of experiential components is one more critical example from flourishing malls. Past the value-based nature of shopping, effective edifices focus on making essential encounters. Whether through indoor carnivals, far-reaching developments, or intuitive display areas, the accentuation on experiential retail lines up with the advancing assumptions for customers who look for something other than items - they want accounts, associations, and improving experiences during their shopping encounters.

Versatility is a foundation illustration got from flourishing retail plazas. The capacity to distinguish and answer shifts in customer conduct, mechanical progressions, and social inclinations guarantees supported pertinence. Flourishing malls influence innovation for accommodation and availability, consolidating computerized wayfinding frameworks, brilliant stopping arrangements, and intelligent presentations. The versatility likewise reaches out to inhabitant blend, with fruitful edifices finding some kind of harmony between laid out extravagance brands, high-road retailers, arising originators, and experiential ideas.

Vital area arises as a significant variable adding to the outcome of flourishing malls. Shopping center of America's essential situating close to a worldwide air terminal adds to its status as a worldwide vacationer location. The illustration here is that area ought to line up with the objective segment and exploit nearby and worldwide the travel industry patterns. Vital situation upgrades perceivability, people walking through, and generally speaking openness, adding to the supported outcome of a retail plaza.

Furthermore, flourishing malls perceive the meaning of local area commitment. Laying out a feeling of local area includes drawing in guests as well as cultivating an association with the nearby people. Occasions, social drives, and joint efforts with nearby organizations add to a feeling of spot, situating the retail plaza as a focal center point inside the local area. The example here is that effective malls stretch out past being business spaces; they become energetic centers that improve the existences of the people who visit and add to the texture of the networks they possess.

Alternately, battling malls offer significant examples by featuring expected entanglements and difficulties in the retail scene. One normal issue looked by striving retail outlets is an absence of versatility. Inability to distinguish and answer changing customer ways of behaving, mechanical progressions, and social movements can prompt out of date quality. Malls that oppose development and stay unbending in their methodology risk losing pertinence and neglecting to meet the advancing assumptions for shoppers.

An illustration from battling malls is the significance of a strong and alluring inhabitant blend. On the off chance that a mall neglects to organize a different scope of retailers that enticement for its objective segment, it might battle to draw in people strolling through. This example highlights the requirement for an intensive comprehension of customer inclinations and market patterns. Neglecting to adjust the occupant blend to the developing requests of the ideal interest group can bring about a decrease in fame and, eventually, monetary difficulties.

Besides, battling retail outlets frequently wrestle with the effect of internet business and changing shopper inclinations. The ascent of web based shopping has reshaped the retail scene, and malls that don't embrace an omnichannel approach might confront hardships. The illustration here is the significance of coordinating computerized systems, like web-based presence, snap and-gather administrations, and other online business drives, to supplement the in-person shopping experience.

One more illustration from battling retail outlets is the likely adverse consequence of a poor actual climate. In the event that a retail outlet needs tasteful allure, neatness, and an inviting climate, it might battle to draw in and hold guests. Feel assume a pivotal part in forming the character of a retail plaza and impacting the general client experience. Ignoring the actual climate can add to a decrease in people walking through and the impression of the retail plaza as an unappealing objective.

Moreover, battling retail plazas frequently face difficulties connected with unfortunate administration and functional failures. Incapable showcasing methodologies, deficient support, and an absence of local area commitment can all add to a decrease in the middle's prosperity. The illustration here is major areas of strength for that, viable administration rehearses, and a pledge to functional greatness are fundamental for the supported outcome of a mall.

The effect of monetary slumps is one more example gathered from battling malls. Monetary vacillations can altogether influence purchaser ways of managing money, and malls that don't expect or adjust to these progressions might confront monetary difficulties. The illustration is the significance of monetary flexibility and possibility intending to effectively explore financial vulnerabilities.

Taking everything into account, the examples gained from both flourishing and battling retail plazas offer significant bits of knowledge for industry partners. Flourishing malls represent the significance of expansion, experiential retail, flexibility, key area, and local area commitment. These variables add to their supported accomplishment as energetic objections that take care of the developing requirements of buyers.

On the other hand, battling malls feature potential traps connected with an absence of flexibility, unfortunate inhabitant blend, the effect of web based business, disregard of the actual climate, the board difficulties, and weakness to monetary slumps. Understanding these difficulties gives a chance to battling malls to reevaluate their procedures, make fundamental changes, and position themselves for future achievement.

At last, the retail scene is a dynamic and serious field where illustrations from both achievement and difficulties make ready for proceeded with development and development. By applying these examples, malls can explore the intricacies of the cutting edge retail climate, live up to the assumptions of knowing purchasers, and make objections that flourish industrially as well as contribute emphatically to the networks they serve.

## 9.3 Final thoughts on the future of shopping centers and their role in the retail indu

The eventual fate of retail outlets remains at the convergence of mechanical advancement, developing purchaser ways of behaving, and dynamic metropolitan scenes. As we ponder the direction of these retail spaces, it becomes obvious that their job in the retail business is ready for change. In these last contemplations, we'll investigate key contemplations molding the eventual fate of malls and the urgent job they play in the more extensive retail scene.

The consistent incorporation of innovation, right off the bat, is vital to the future progress of retail plazas. The computerized domain, incorporating web based business, versatile applications, and online stages, has reshaped customer assumptions. Malls should adjust by embracing mechanical arrangements that improve the general client experience, both on the web and disconnected. From shrewd stopping frameworks and computerized wayfinding to expanded reality applications that work with virtual attempt ons, the combination of innovation lifts comfort, commitment, and personalization.

The ascent of web based business has provoked a change in perspective in how buyers approach retail, and malls should situate themselves as corresponding to this computerized scene. An omnichannel approach, where on the web and disconnected channels are consistently interconnected, becomes basic. Retail plazas can use their actual spaces as centers for snap and-gather administrations, experiential display areas, and occasions that overcome any issues between the virtual and actual domains. This crossover model recognizes the significance of both on the web and in-person shopping encounters, taking special care of the inclinations of different customer portions.

Additionally, the fate of malls is characteristically connected to the idea of experiential retail. Past the value-based nature of buying merchandise, customers look for essential encounters that reverberate with their way of life and values. Fruitful malls will organize conditions that go past the conventional retail model, consolidating diversion, comprehensive developments, and vivid attractions. The combination of retail and diversion makes an objective where guests spend on items as well as on encounters, encouraging a feeling of association and steadfastness.

The job of maintainability coming soon for retail plazas couldn't possibly be more significant. As natural awareness turns out to be progressively essential to buyer independent direction, retail plazas should take on eco-accommodating practices. This incorporates supportable engineering, energy-productive innovations, squander decrease drives, and a guarantee to moral obtaining. Green spaces, eco-accommodating plans, and an emphasis on dependable utilization contribute not exclusively to natural stewardship yet in addition to the allure of retail plazas for socially cognizant shoppers.

Moreover, the future outcome of retail outlets relies on their capacity to act as powerful spaces inside advancing metropolitan scenes. As urban areas go through changes driven by segment shifts, mechanical headways, and changing work designs, retail plazas should adjust to these movements. Nearness to travel center points, key situating inside blended use improvements, and a profound mix into the texture of metropolitan life are fundamental contemplations. The future retail plaza isn't simply an objective yet a basic piece of the metropolitan experience, adding to the essentialness and network of the encompassing local area.

The developing job of information examination and man-made reasoning is a critical thought for the fate of retail outlets. Outfitting the force of information permits malls to acquire important bits of knowledge into purchaser conduct, inclinations, and patterns. This information driven approach illuminates key direction, from occupant choice and promoting procedures to customized client encounters. Computerized reasoning, through prescient examination and AI, empowers malls to expect and adjust to changing business sector elements, guaranteeing readiness and seriousness in the retail scene.

The development of brilliant urban communities and the Web of Things (IoT) presents extra open doors for malls later on. Availability and interoperability with shrewd city framework can upgrade the general insight for guests. From shrewd stopping arrangements that advance traffic stream to IoT-empowered sensors that give continuous information on people strolling through and buyer inclinations, the combination of savvy innovations positions retail plazas as essential parts of cutting edge metropolitan environments.

The eventual fate of malls likewise includes a reconsidering of the customary retail rent model. Adaptable and versatile renting designs will turn out to be more common, permitting retailers to explore different avenues regarding new ideas, spring up shops, and inventive joint efforts. This adaptability answers the developing idea of retail and encourages a climate where inventiveness and business flourish. The ease of renting courses of action empowers retail plazas to stay dynamic and receptive to arising patterns.

As we imagine the eventual fate of malls, perceiving the proceeded with significance of human-driven design is fundamental. While innovation assumes a significant part, the actual climate of retail plazas stays a focal figure molding the general client experience. Smart engineering, engaging feel, and an emphasis on making inviting and agreeable spaces add to the close to home association among buyers and retail plazas. The harmony among innovation and a human-driven approach characterizes the progress of future retail spaces.

All in all, the eventual fate of malls is a scene of development, variation, and change. Mechanical reconciliation, experiential retail, supportability rehearses, metropolitan availability, information examination, and adaptable renting models are key parts that will shape the direction of malls before long. As these retail spaces advance, they are not just areas for exchanges but rather unique center points that add to the social, social, and monetary texture of the networks they serve.

The flexibility and versatility of malls will be tried as they explore the difficulties and amazing open doors introduced by an always changing retail scene. By embracing advancement, focusing on customer encounters, and lining up with more extensive cultural movements, malls can situate themselves as energetic and irreplaceable supporters representing things to come of retail. As the excursion unfurls, the effective malls of tomorrow will be those that embrace change, expect patterns, and keep on rethinking the limits of what a retail objective can be.

The eventual fate of malls holds a critical job in the consistently developing scene of the retail business. As we look forward, it becomes obvious that retail plazas are not simple actual spaces for exchanges but rather unique center points that shape and answer arising patterns, innovative progressions, and changing customer ways of behaving. In these reflections on the fate of malls, we investigate the complex aspects that will characterize their job in the retail business.

At the core representing things to come of retail plazas is the extraordinary impact of innovation. The advanced upset has reshaped the manner in which purchasers associate with retail, and malls should embrace mechanical combination to stay pertinent. The ascent of internet business and the commonness of web based shopping have tested the conventional physical model. Malls that influence innovation to upgrade the general client experience won't just get by yet flourish in this computerized period.

One of the key innovative contemplations is the consistent coordination of on the web and disconnected channels, known as the omnichannel approach. Malls representing things to come should perceive that shoppers frequently draw in with brands across different touchpoints. The actual mall turns into a center point for encounters, supplemented by an internet based presence that works with comfort, openness, and a customized venture for every customer. An amicable exchange between the physical and computerized domains makes a comprehensive retail biological system.

Besides, the consolidation of state of the art innovations inside malls adds to a more vivid and connecting with client experience. From expanded reality (AR) applications that empower virtual attempt ons to brilliant mirrors giving continuous item data, innovation turns into an empowering agent of accommodation and personalization. The mix of computerized wayfinding frameworks and portable applications smoothes out the shopping venture, offering guests a consistent route insight inside the sweeping bounds of malls.

The ascent of experiential retail arises as a principal trait representing things to come mall. Past filling in as simple storehouses of items, effective malls curate conditions that offer paramount encounters. Amusement, comprehensive developments, and vivid attractions become basic parts of the retail outlet's allure. Customers look for products as well as a feeling of association and commitment, and malls that get it and answer this want will flourish later on retail scene.

Supportability remains as a center guideline forming the fate of retail outlets. With natural cognizance turning into a focal thought for customers, retail outlets should embrace eco-accommodating practices. Feasible engineering, energy-effective innovations, squander decrease drives, and a promise to moral obtaining are basic components. Green spaces and eco-accommodating plans contribute not exclusively to natural stewardship yet in addition to the engaging quality of malls for socially cognizant purchasers.

The essential job of retail plazas inside metropolitan scenes is one more huge part of their future. As urban communities go through changes affected by segment shifts, mechanical progressions, and changing work designs, retail outlets should adjust to these movements. Closeness to travel center points, coordination into blended use improvements, and a profound association with the metropolitan texture are fundamental contemplations. Retail outlets become independent objections as well as basic parts of the metropolitan experience, adding to the essentialness and availability of the encompassing local area.

The developing scene of information examination and computerized reasoning (man-made intelligence) adds a layer of refinement to the eventual fate of retail outlets. The capacity to saddle information for bits of knowledge into buyer conduct, inclinations, and patterns turns into an upper hand. Information driven direction illuminates all that from occupant choice and advertising systems to customized client encounters. Man-made consciousness, through prescient examination and AI, engages retail plazas to expect and adjust to changing business sector elements, guaranteeing nimbleness and seriousness.

The rise of shrewd urban areas and the Web of Things (IoT) presents extra open doors for malls later on. Network and interoperability with shrewd city foundation can upgrade the general insight for guests. Shrewd stopping arrangements improving traffic stream, IoT-empowered sensors giving continuous information on people strolling through, and customized proposals in view of customer conduct are signs of the advantageous connection between malls and brilliant city biological systems.

The future of renting models is likewise going through a change in outlook. The customary long haul rent model is giving way to additional adaptable and versatile plans. Malls perceive the need to oblige the powerful idea of retail by offering more limited leases, spring up spaces, and open doors for inventive joint efforts. This adaptability draws in a different scope of retailers as well as encourages a climate where imagination and business can thrive.

Human-driven plan stays a focal thought coming soon for retail plazas. While innovation assumes a significant part, the actual climate of retail plazas keeps on molding the general client experience. Smart engineering, engaging style, and an emphasis on making inviting and agreeable spaces add to the close to home association among purchasers and malls. Finding some kind of harmony among innovation and a human-driven approach characterizes the outcome of future retail spaces.

All in all, the eventual fate of retail plazas is a juncture of development, variation, and change. Mechanical joining, experiential retail, maintainability rehearses, metropolitan network, information examination, adaptable renting models, and human-driven plan are key parts that will shape the direction of malls before long. These retail spaces are not just ready to get by in a computerized period yet to flourish as dynamic supporters of the social, social, and financial texture of the networks they serve.

The flexibility and versatility of malls will be tried as they explore the difficulties and open doors introduced by a consistently changing retail scene. By embracing advancement, focusing on purchaser encounters, and lining up with more extensive cultural movements, malls can situate themselves as imperative supporters representing things to come of retail. As the excursion unfurls, the fruitful malls of tomorrow will be those that embrace change, expect patterns, and keep on rethinking the limits of what a retail objective can be.

www.ingramcontent.com/pod-product-compliance
Lightning Source LLC
LaVergne TN
LVHW010219070526
838199LV00062B/4661